GUAC IS EXTRA
BUT SO AM I

THE RELUCTANT
ADULT'S HANDBOOK

TEXT AND ILLUSTRATIONS BY

SARAH SOLOMON

powerHouse Books
BROOKLYN, NY

Dedicated to Grandma Eleanor,
the only person who willfully refuses
to acknowledge any of my bad qualities.
I love you more than words can ever express.

Please skip over most of these chapters.

Table of Contents

INTRODUCTION

Can I still hail an Uber on the road less traveled?

If I could describe my early twenties in two words, it would probably be, "screaming internally."

You're starting a new chapter in your life that's drastically different from the ones before. For many of you, it's the first time you'll truly be on your own without the benefit and convenience of having college friends around or a set schedule with end points and dates clearly marked and labeled. Now what?

Applying for your first job, and not screwing up when you finally land an interview, is a feat in itself. Deciphering the nuances of office politics is its own animal, and don't even get me started on personal relationships in uncharted digital waters where your soul mate could be a right swipe away. Dealing with personal finances is "fun," too.

But the good news is, you can do it. You never know what you're capable of until you have to rise to the occasion, and you will pleasantly surprise yourself. Plus, you're going to have a hell of a lot of fun doing so.

This book will go over some of the things that people expect you to either inherently know or pick up along the way, but I've laid it out for you because subtlety was never in my wheelhouse. Topics range from how to pack up your apartment and move everything you own, to dinner etiquette that'll come in handy when you're dealing with business clients. Aside from the benefit of my experience (and screw ups!), there's a ton of advice from friends and professionals who know the answers because they lived through it.

The last chapter contains life advice from people that have it all together and are killing it in their respective fields, addressed to their younger selves. While I cannot claim such a feat, I'd be remiss to not include my own thoughts here, for a recently graduated Sarah.

NOTES TO MY YOUNGER SELF

There's something to be said about living in the moment—because time is linear and you'll never be as young and cute as you are right now, blah, blah, blah—but just relax and know it's all going to get easier and better. As the years progress, your standards improve along with your paycheck and you become more certain about your wants, needs, and goals.

Now I've got some good news and bad news, but because I know you have anxiety, let's get the bad news over with first.

SOME OF THE HARDER TRUTHS:

THERE NEVER WAS AND NEVER WILL BE A LEVEL PLAYING FIELD

Someone's parents are going to call their friend at the company and get their kid that job you wanted. You never know whose parents are still paying their rent and credit card bill until you walk into their glorious one-bedroom apartment bereft of Craigslist roommates. Someone will have an insanely cool job because they can afford to live off a crappy salary that unfortunately complements some of the creative professions. Accept this and work your ass off regardless, because "life isn't fair" is more than a universal truth—it's a day-to-day existence.

SOME PEOPLE AREN'T GOING TO LIKE YOU

And it's OK! You're probably not going to like them either. It's better to be an acquired taste than a generic copy of what is socially acceptable. There's something to be said about unapologetically being yourself, especially in the face of adversity—or a work nemesis.

THINGS WON'T WORK OUT AS PLANNED

You will go through the motions and do everything that was recommended and looks good on paper and still be passed over or lose opportunities that rightfully should have been yours. While this is easier said than done, accept it, learn from it, and move on. Play the long game.

YOU'RE NOT THAT SPECIAL

I mean, I think you're great aside from the things you did and said that still make you cringe as they play on repeat in your head when you can't sleep, but just acknowledge that there's literally thousands of people that can do what you do, and do it better. Respect that.

AND NOW FOR THE GOOD NEWS:

You will get savvier and stronger. While not physically (uhh, sorry about that) then at least emotionally and professionally. You will overcome hurdles, and experience triumphs, loves, and losses. You will build up everything you thought was correct and then burn it all down, rising like a phoenix from the ashes of Ben Affleck's terrible midlife crisis tattoo.

To quote the late, great Joan Rivers, "Listen. I wish I could tell you it gets better. But, it doesn't get better. You get better."

CHAPTER 1

Feigning Adulthood

The Bare Minimum Cheat Sheet

"Matching pajamas allow you to feel like you have some semblance of your life together," she said to the stray cat. It blankly looked at her.

A wise man or woman that has been plagiarized throughout the years famously said, "There are no shortcuts in life." That person was either comfortable being a dirty, filthy liar or wasn't admitting they got their internship through family friends.

Life has a tricky way of managing to become taxing, even if things appear to be going smoothly on the surface. Even with a family in good health, decent job, and significant other, you still have to wake up every morning and go through the motions of being a contributing member of society. This can be exhausting on its own.

It's important to find your own twisted path through life, but here are some basic tips and tricks for efficient coasting that helps leave time and funds for other things you enjoy. Whether that's sports, traveling, or getting overinvolved with reality TV stars' lives—I leave that in your (somewhat) capable hands.

The apartment or home essentials you didn't know you needed (or could leave out).

To really make a house a home, or your apartment something less spartan and more livable, you need the basic necessities. That means you need the stuff necessary for you to comfortably cook, entertain, or simply enjoy an afternoon in the space you're paying for without having a deep personal crisis over only owning plastic takeout cutlery.

Kitchen Essentials

We live in the golden age of convenient appliances, especially if you've got money to burn. Because space is usually at a premium in urban apartments, you have to pick and choose what you want/need/drunkenly order from Amazon while lamenting the cost of constant takeout.

None of the below non-essential but useful kitchen items take up a ton of space on their own, but it's worth noting that an excessive number of appliances can quickly become little more than clutter. The last thing you need are kitchen cabinets that spontaneously burst under the metaphorical and tangible weight of your new culinary aspirations. You might feel differently after a weekend of doing nothing but binge-watching competitive cooking shows, but resist the urge and quiet your inner-chef, at least until you've slept a night on everything patiently waiting in your online shopping cart.

Going to start referring to my apart-ment as my pied-à-terre to falsely imply that I have somewhere, anywhere else to go.

NON-NEGOTIABLES

- Cutting board
- Knife set (paring knife, serrated knife, chef's knife)
- Measuring cups and spoons
- Can opener
- Large pot
- Colander
- Non-stick skillet (extra points for a cast-iron pan)
- Potholders
- Matching wine glasses
- Baking sheet
- Spices and oils
- Serving bowl
- Full set of utensils
- Aluminum foil and Saran or waxed wrap

"I've really gotten into urban farming."

"Buying a basil plant at Trader Joe's doesn't count."

CROCKPOT

A crockpot is a magical creation that slow-cooks whatever the hell you want, at a low enough temperature you can leave it on overnight or when you go to work. They range from cheaper iterations that you have to unplug to stop, self-timed ones, or more advanced options you can control via an app. Because the Internet has apparently come for your chili.

They're quite magical year round, ranging from supplying hearty winter stews to allowing you to sometimes forego the summertime dread of turning on the oven. There's nothing like walking into your home after work and smelling dinner already made—because instant gratification is necessary after staring at countless Excel sheets all day.

CHAMPAGNE STOPPER

Champagne, unlike most alcoholic social lubricants, has the tendency to go bad after uncorking. Rather than wasting that precious, precious fizz, invest in a champagne stopper for as little as $7 and keep popping that existential dread away. There's a bootleg hack involving adding raisins to your champagne flute but it's all a dirty lie.

SPIRALIZER

Albeit painfully trendy, spiralizers are quite useful. They make quick work of creating vegetable pasta (sorry, not sorry—zoodles aren't that bad) or slivered potatoes for hash browns.

SOUS VIDE

Unlike grilling or broiling meat, a sous vide cooks your dish at an exact temperature for a precise amount of time so you don't have to worry about checking internal temperatures. It's like idiot-proofing your meat or fish.

PITCHER

Invaluable for serving drinks as they were meant to be served—en masse. Ideally you'll have both ceramic and glass pitchers because if you're hosting brunch you'll already need one for coffee and another for mimosas. They also come in handy as vases or someplace to hide prescription drugs from your roommate's sketchy app date.

COCKTAIL NAPKINS/COASTERS

Even if you couldn't care less about your IKEA coffee table that has been through far too much, or your apartment has granite countertop as far as the eye can see, coasters are still a nice, noticeable addition. Like all accent pieces they provide a chance to show off some of your personality or become an opportunity to monogram the shit out of something.

BLENDER

From soups to dips to drinks, blenders are really worth their weight in protein smoothies. While not all of us need the Cadillac of blenders, the blades have to be sharp enough to cut through enough ice to make margaritas so you don't end up throwing it out the window in hungover frustration.

COFFEE MAKER

Never discount the number of times you'll thank you coffee maker, especially when you're broke and don't feel like blowing $2+ every time you need a caffeine fix.

There are so many levels of decent coffee makers, you can get one for as little as $10 if you're in a bind, or go up in quality and design from there. You also have to consider whether you want a French press, an app-controlled machine, a pour-over brewer, but for the love of God don't get one that makes your brew from pods. You can use a Keurig ad nauseum at work, but life is too short to start your morning with apathy for both the environment and the quality of your coffee.

DECENT TUPPERWARE

Old Chinese takeout containers only go so far, and if you're carting meals in your work tote you want something that securely locks so it doesn't unceremoniously dump all over your bag.

HOW TO SEASON AND MAINTAIN YOUR CAST-IRON SKILLET

Cast-iron skillets can become the most versatile tools in your kitchen—not to mention they're trendy as hell and make you seem both utilitarian and elitist all at once.

Cast-iron doesn't like three things:

- High-acid foods (like citrus or vinegar)
- Soap
- Water

This means you can't stick your skillet in the dishwasher or cook acidic foods with it. You've probably heard cast-iron nerds talking about seasoning their skillet like it's

"He really took your lumberjack fetish joke to heart, didn't he?"

some holy ritual. However, even a novice such as yourself shouldn't be afraid to jump in—seasoning the skillet is the same process whether it's brand new or you're a kitchen veteran. The more you use your cast-iron pan, the more seasoned and better it will become.

Step 1: Pour some vegetable oil in the skillet, rubbing it all over the interior with a towel. If it's a new skillet, you'll want to rub off the coating supplied by the manufacturer. Continue applying and rubbing until there's no more gunk or unspeakable detritus left on your towel.

Step 2: Baking time. Stick your skillet in the oven for an hour at 350 degrees. Once it's cooled off, repeat the vegetable oil rubbing routine—if the towel is clean, you're done.

If the towel isn't clean, continue repeating steps one and two until it is. No one likes a filthy skillet. This should get easier and more rewarding as time goes on.

"Why do you have your grocery list tacked to your vision board?"

"Do you not find cheese plates inspirational?"

GROCERIES TO ALWAYS HAVE ON HAND

So, what should you always have in your kitchen? Only you can be the judge of that, but you should always have some items, both perishable and not, that allow you to easily and mindlessly cobble together meals that aren't instant ramen or a sleeve of Oreos.

Some bare necessities:

- Olive oil
- Vegetable oil
- Salt
- Pepper
  Various spices
- Bread
- Eggs
- Pasta sauce
- Pasta
- Peanut butter and jelly
- Lemon juice
- Onions
- Garlic
- Chickpeas
- Black beans
- Potatoes
- Salsa (can also be used as salad dressing or marinade in a pinch)
- Canned tuna
- Cheese
- Chicken
- Greens
- Fruits
- Vegetables
- Chicken or soup stock
- Bagged salad mix

From just those items, you can make a hell of a lot of meals. Cooking forces you to eat healthier, and you'll be disturbed by how much money you're saving by cutting back on takeout.

"911, what's your emergency?"

A HANDY GUIDE TO EXPIRATION DATES

Ah yes, the elusive fridge gamble. We've all done the tentative sniff to see if the milk is still good, or spat out a rotten orange slice because time is a cyclical pattern of abuse that pauses for no one.

Everything should be suspect to suspicion, but here's, generally speaking, when groceries go bad in your fridge.

- **Eggs:** up to a month
- **Cheese:** two to four months
- **Milk:** up to a week
- **Yogurt:** up to three weeks
- **Bacon:** up to two weeks but can be frozen up to 4 months
- **Chicken:** up to two days but can be frozen up to a year
- **Fish:** up to two days but can be frozen for six to nine months
- **Hamburger and steak:** up to two days but can be frozen for six to eight months
- **Bread:** up to two weeks in the fridge but can be frozen for two to three months

"How many years am I taking off my life by not exclusively buying organic produce?"

PRODUCE

- **Apples:** up to four weeks on the counter, two months in the fridge, and up to a year in the freezer
- **Bananas:** up to a week on the counter or fridge and three months in the freezer
- **Grapes:** up to five days on the counter, ten days in the fridge, and five months in the freezer
- **Lemons:** up to a month on the counter, two months in the fridge, and four months in the freezer
- **Strawberries:** up to two days on the counter, a week in the fridge, and eight months in the freezer

HOME ESSENTIALS

To maintain the appearance that you don't live in total squalor, behold some of the household items that meet the bare minimum.

- Mattress
- Decent sheets
- Mattress pad
- Duvet cover
- Full-length mirror
- Framed artwork
- Lamps
- Nightstand
- Coffee table
- Decent towels
- Bath mat
- Plunger
- Extra towels and sheets

Eggs

3-4 weeks in the fridge

Bananas

up to 9 days on the Counter
up to 9 days in the fridge
up to 3 months in the freezer

Carrots

up to 4 days on the Counter
up to 5 weeks in the fridge
up to a year in the freezer

Tomatoes

up to 7 days on the Counter
up to 2 weeks in the fridge
up to a year in the freezer

MILK

up to a week in the fridge

up to a month in the freezer

Bacon

up to 2 weeks in the fridge

up to 4 months in the freezer

Bread

up to a week on the Counter
up to 2 weeks in the fridge
up to 3 months in the freezer

Hard Cheese

up to 3 months on the Counter
up to 4 months in the fridge
up to 8 months in the freezer

The road to hell is paved with shag carpeting.

EXTRA ESSENTIALS

PULL-OUT SOFA/AIR MATTRESS

Your friends deserve better than the floor. If you've inherited or acquired a sofa that doesn't transform into a bed, spring for a blow up mattress so they don't hate you in the morning (at least more than they usually do).

THROW BLANKET

Ratty fleece throws don't count. Opt for a light blanket you won't mind snuggling with during a movie session that will also tie together the rest of the room, or at least not completely disrupt it. It doesn't have to match the rest of the decor, just complement the overarching theme, such as "cabin-inspired," "suburban hideaway," "urban sprawl," "trust fund treasure," or "may I look back on these days and laugh."

BOX FRAME

Apparently even successful people think having a mattress on the floor is a suitable option (as myself and too many friends have encountered). Raise your damn mattress off your floor, and your standards at the same time.

SHOWER CURTAIN

No, that see-through liner doesn't count. Look like an adult. Be an adult. Buy a tasteful shower curtain that complements your bathroom or amuses you in some capacity. However, that graphic *Psycho*-themed curtain probably isn't a good idea if you're already nervous about scaring off visitors.

TOOL SET

Everyone should have a tool set so you can, you know, fix things. Normally this would include: a hammer and nails, a screwdriver, a tape measure, and screws of various sizes. You should upgrade yours if you actually plan on doing handiwork in your home, and definitely get a good power drill if you're planning on doing any sort of remodeling.

WINE OPENER THAT YOU'RE COMFORTABLE WITH

Unless you're a sommelier or wine mom, you're not steadily uncorking bottle after bottle on the regular. Accidents happen with lesser wine openers, like the ones you can find on swiss army knives or cheap, branded giveaway swag. Get one you can deal with under stress or in front of a crowd—breaking your cork while under duress when you could really use a drink, or during a party, is never fun.

BLACKOUT SHADES

No, these aren't the same as the drunk goggles you put on after a few shots of Fireball during a dry spell. Blackout shades ensure you'll actually get to sleep in on the weekend, aside from any early wake-ups from pets, strangers, and significant others who, too early in the morning, you wish were still strangers.

"I find it disturbing that you named your plant after your ex."

"My therapist recommended yelling at something that can't file a restraining order."

PLANTS

Easy indoor plants have all the benefit of making it look like you can take care of and lovingly cherish a living thing, without admitting that it literally takes the bare minimum for them to survive. Proven mood lifters and an evergreen decoration that complements most aesthetics, these house plant options are both hardy and an exercise in maturity.

ALOE VERA

Why it's cool: You most likely have some creams and ointments with aloe vera as a main ingredient; this guy can be sacrificed when you get burns from the sun or cooking fouls.

What it needs: Lots of sunlight and room temperatures with not too much water.

SUCCULENTS

Why it's cool: You can get succulents anywhere, and they're usually already planted in fun pots because they've been extremely "in" for the past few years.

What they need: Word of warning; the more brightly colored the succulent is (red, orange, yellow etc.) the more light it'll need. Water every few days and keep in the sun.

JADE PLANT

Why it's cool: Like its more popular cousin, the succulent, jade will live for a long time—and unlike your last relationship, will require next to no effort.

What it needs: Sunlight and room temperatures with little water.

Unlike your S.O., a fiddle leaf fig only looks high maintenance!

FIDDLE LEAF FIG

Why it's cool: This uber-trendy tree has beautiful leaves, and only looks high maintenance.

What it needs: Medium to bright light and room temperatures around 65-75° with intermittent watering.

CLEANING YOUR APARTMENT

A clean apartment is a necessity on multiple levels:

YOUR COMFORT

Even if you're used to living in total squalor, coming home to even a cleanish apartment, house, or bedroom is cathartic. Your life tends to feel like it's more in order when there aren't half-drunk Bud Light cans strewn around the apartment like the saddest Easter egg hunt.

TO KEEP UP APPEARANCES

No one will want to hang out at your place if it's a notorious mess. A rule of thumb is to leave your apartment only in such a state of disarray that it takes five-ish minutes to clean up if you have unexpected guests on the way. Unfortunately you can't guarantee that any roommates will adhere to a similar hard-and-fast rule, but you can at least make them feel guilty about it by keeping your own area clean, doing the dishes, picking up after yourself, and other examples of considerate behavior—passive-aggressively refusing to clean the common spaces doesn't help anyone.

MATURITY

We're all in a constant state of evolution, but a clean space helps you think that you're further along the "mature choices" train than you are, and may even compel you to make better decisions. Waking up and not being able to see the floor of your room, even if you don't particularly mind it, can eventually become demoralizing. You deserve a clean, healthy space without filth or the critters that will be attracted to it.

CLEANING TIPS

Cleaning your apartment or home may seem like a Sisyphean effort—it'll clearly just get dirty again—but if you make it into a mindless weekly routine then it becomes a less painful habit. I hate to say it but, as I've gotten older, cleaning has become therapeutic, if only because I know the end result will make me happy. A clean home is a somewhat sane home, or at the very least one that won't make you question your sanity as you attempt to take a week's worth of takeout boxes to the recycling.

A few rules of thumb:

DUST, VACUUM, AND GO OVER YOUR SURFACES WEEKLY

By going over your surfaces every week with a cleaning solution and cloth, vacuuming, or using antibacterial reinforcements in the kitchen and bathroom area, you've already done a lot of the heavy lifting. *Weekly maintenance will save you many hours down the road*, when you realize you have to get a quarter inch of accumulated scum off everything you once knew and loved.

MAKE SURE YOUR TUB AND TOILET ARE SPARKLING WHITE

One of the biggest turn-offs is going into someone's bathroom and the toilet and tub reveal what a disgusting creature they actually are. Don't be that person.

TOILET TALK (I APOLOGIZE IN ADVANCE)

Owning a plunger, toilet brush, and toilet cleaning solution are non-negotiables. The cleaning solution should save you some heavy scrubbing, and the toilet brush and plunger should be self-explanatory. If you need to plunge your toilet and the water is rising steadily—turn off the damn water by turning the knob at the back of the toilet before attempting anything.

Take the plunger and make sure it aligns with the hole of the toilet and give it three or four swift pumps until you can feel the suction. If the water disappears or you feel comfortable with the water level, turn the knob to bring the water back on and flush.

In a perfect world you should be cleaning your toilet weekly, going over every part of its surface. Even the stand of the toilet deserves a scrub down, as it tends to accumulate hair and every manner of filth we won't discuss.

TUB SCRUB

Cleaning your tub is yet another distasteful venture into maturity you should be attempting. If there's mildew and scum coating the surface—it may be time to break out the bleach. Measure ¼ to ½ cup for every gallon of water, put that mixture in a spray bottle, and go to town with a scrub brush. **Do not** mix bleach with ammonia or other cleaners. It could literally kill you.

If you don't need bleach, you can attack the tub with any bathroom cleaning solutions that promise shiny, white surfaces. It may feel counterintuitive to have to regularly clean the item that rinses you off, but it's just another unfortunate reality of being an adult.

There's nothing like deep-cleaning your apartment to avoid the other much more intimidating items on your to-do list.

CHANGE YOUR SHEETS EVERY TWO WEEKS
A fresh pair of sheets is a total game changer. Not only does it feel great and leave you with that clean, responsible feeling, but it's so much better for your skin. If you're getting laid a lot (congratulations, by the way), you should probably be changing them more often.

GET A CORDLESS VACUUM
You don't want to be that person who only vacuums as far as the cord will go. Make life easier on yourself and opt for something that won't get tangled.

YES, YOU CAN WASH A DOWN COMFORTER
It will probably just take up the entirety of your washer and take a while to dry. If you're looking to deal with something a little lighter, a duvet cover is easier to clean and sometimes cheaper to boot. Don't forget to occasionally wash your pillows as well.

DO NOT WASH AND DRY YOUR DARKS AND LIGHTS TOGETHER TO SAVE MONEY
The darker items will rub off onto your whites, thereby eradicating any savings when you have to replace all your (now pink) tighty whities.

DON'T THROW EVERYTHING IN THE DRYER
Your delicates (which you should be washing in a mesh garment bag) should NEVER go in the dryer, along with non-iron dress shirts, wool sweaters, or anything that can shrink and ruin your day. Hang up your dress shirts—I suggest velvet hangers because plastic hangers are the devil's plaything—and lay your sweaters flat out to dry so you don't stretch out the shoulders.

CONSIDER CLEANING CLOTHS
Paper towels take up a ton of room, are an added expense, and really not that great for the environment. Enter cleaning cloths that you can reuse after washing and take the guilt out of filling an entire trash can with paper towels after an "Oh dear God, when was the last time I dusted?" spree.

CLEAN YOUR WASHING MACHINE AND DISHWASHER
It may seem strange to clean your cleaning tools, but so much gunk will build up in them over time it could defeat their whole purpose. Thankfully, you can easily clean both your dishwasher and washing machine by respectively running them on empty with white vinegar and wiping them down afterwards.

Run your dishwasher and washing machine on hot with a glass of vinegar on the top rack of the dishwasher and dump a cup or two of white vinegar into the washing machine. After they've finished their respective cycles, wipe clean and feel smugly satisfied with how much of an adult you are.

FRIENDSHIPS—THEY GET HARDER

One of the hardest parts about graduating and moving to a new city is starting over, especially in the friend department. Even though it's easy to stay in touch with old friends no matter the distance, it's hard to accept that you can't walk a few blocks to their apartment, and will not see them for months at time. It really and truly sucked for me and I was in a funk about it for about a year because all my college friends stayed in Philadelphia and I felt severely alone.

I met most of my NYC friends through Twitter and jobs I held. *I can't say enough good things about meeting people IRL that you connected with through Twitter and Instagram and the like*—if you enjoy what they're saying in a limited context you'll probably like them even more in person. Granted, this was in 2011 before *everyone* had social media so it was easier to identify and connect with people I would get along with. Lo and behold, nearly a decade later, they're still some of my closest friends.

Emily Stewart, a writer for *Vox* and a dear friend I met through a previous employer, has had a lot of experience with living in drastically different places and making new friends. She suggested:

> "Say yes to everything. Literally everything. (Within reason—don't, you know, agree to assist in a murder.) But whenever someone invites you to do something or go somewhere, no matter how tired you are, or how unappealing or nerve-wracking it sounds, go. It will help with some of the new-city loneliness, and it's really a good way to meet potential new friends.
>
> You also have to be a little more forgiving of and open to the people you do meet. When I was living in Buenos Aires, I wound up befriending some people I probably wouldn't have been friends with in 'real life'—as in, in the United States. That's OK.
>
> And, if you're up for it, liquid courage is helpful. I had a friend who took salsa classes in Medellin to meet people and definitely had a couple of drinks ahead of time. It helped."

If you're looking to meet new people, consider joining community sports teams (which are basically just drinking leagues), young professionals networking groups, philanthropic efforts...whatever your interests, there's probably a young members' version of it.

DON'T PANIC WHEN SOME FRIENDSHIPS FALL TO THE WAYSIDE

Did you know that every seven to ten years, nearly all the cells in your body replace themselves? For all intents and purposes, you are literally a new person every decade. And so are your friends. Careers, significant others, the stress of not having enough time or finances to travel and see them, all of these factors weigh heavily on relationships.

Do your best to stay in touch and see the people you love whenever you can, but don't beat yourself up if you can't see some of your older friends as

"It's exhausting pretending some of your friends' babies are cute."

much as you used to or aren't texting with them as frequently.

That running joke about how nobody talks about Jesus' miracle of having 12 close friends in his 30s hits the nail on the head. Your priorities change as you get older and it gets harder to balance commitments when there are other people who depend on you (like your significant other, aging parents, or maybe even kids) in the mix.

CALL YOUR FAMILY

Your family loves you, and as much as you may not want to go into graphic detail about what you did over the weekend (Mom, can I bleach Jell-O stains out of a sundress?), they want to hear from you.

I'm going to refrain from getting into how to deal with familial relationships because everyone's family is drastically different, but as the years go on, the realization that your grandparents, parents, and siblings are all irrevocably getting older is a painful one. Spend time with and talk to the people you love while you still can.

WHEN IT'S UNFAIR TO GET A PET

Pets are great! Taking care of a pet is in some ways like getting a small, furry child that doesn't have to inherit all of your bad qualities. They can be your devoted friend and companion for life, not to mention the equivalent of a fluffy therapist.

All of my high school era play- lists are a great reminder of why I wasn't popular in high school.

However, as much as you may desperately want a pet, sometimes being a real adult is asking yourself the hard questions. Like, can you adequately take care of another living, feeling, relatively defenseless creature besides yourself? Do you have the funds, living space, and time?

If this is a joint venture by you and your significant other to test the waters of how well you mesh when dealing with an important life step (that is not a child), then you can divvy up the work and it gets somewhat easier. But then there's the quagmire of who gets ownership if you two split up.

Other things to consider are: How much will your utilities go up if you need to keep the air or heat on all day for a pet? Will they shed? Does your residence allow pets (if you're renting)? Is this a passing fancy or are you convinced that you desperately need an animal in your life?

In terms of additional costs, there's pet insurance, vet bills, medication, cleaning supplies, food, boarding costs when you go on vacation, various outfits they'll hate but it's Halloween and you need Instagram fodder—the list goes on and on.

As much as it sucks, you may come to the realization that you can barely make it through the week yourself, and it would be unfair to the animal if they're stuck in your apartment all day while you're at work. On the bright side, you can dog- or cat-sit your friends' pets for free without dealing with the trials of full ownership.

If you realize that you in fact can afford a pet and have the time and space for one, consider adoption before buying from a breeder. Giving a needy animal a home is one of the best things you can do in this world.

Does "do one thing a day that scares you" include checking voicemails from your parents?

MOVING

They say three of the most stressful things in life are to lose a loved one (either to the Great Beyond or their former intern), moving, and starting a new job. At the moment, we're going to discuss the personal hell that is moving.

There are a few ways to go about this depending on where you're moving and what you're willing to spend. If you want to use a broker they can take a fee anywhere from the equivalent of one month's rent to 15% of the rent for the year. If a broker gets you into a building sans fee, then their cost is sometimes tacked into the rent without you knowing it.

If you want to snag a place without a broker, speak to management companies for buildings that meet your specifications, or look up apartments or buildings that rent from the owner.

If you're moving to a new city or can't take the time off work to search for an apartment (competition can be disturbingly fierce for apartments that don't necessitate a broker's fee, at least in New York), then a broker is definitely a good idea. You want to like your home and your neighborhood—the

"Waste not, want not," she said to her cat, finishing a glass of wine from last night. The cat was disinterested, she had seen her do worse.

alternative is too depressing—so the broker's cost is almost a moot point.

Let's fast-forward past the hours, days, and weeks of your life you'll never get back to apartment hunting and dive into moving!

Moving costs and building fees quickly add up, especially if you're dealing with a luxury building. For example, buildings can charge for the following:

- Application fee
- Credit check
- Moving fee

Why am I paying so much in rent considering the amount of time I live in my own head?

...and this is *on top* of first month's and last month's rent, plus a security deposit.

When you go about hiring movers, it's best to find them via word of mouth, but look for the most highly-rated options online and get quotes from a few different companies. And *definitely* read the fine print so you're not shelling out for unnecessary packaging, equipment, or fees you didn't know were involved.

Movers can potentially charge for:

- Packing
- Packing supplies
- Any tickets they acquire while parking or driving
- Overtime

If you don't want to buy cardboard boxes that you'll have to eventually break down and recycle, you can rent stackable boxes that will be picked up afterwards by the box company. It may not be the most economical but it helps cut down on stress and is more environmentally friendly. Or try asking your local bodega if they have any boxes they're getting rid of and use those.

If you're planning on moving yourself or asking friends to help, just remember that no one wants to spend their day moving heavy furniture and compensate the helpers with at least food and/or booze.

PACKING TIPS

Moving is going to suck no matter what, and there's nothing you can really do to mitigate that besides:

> A) planning and packing as far ahead as possible, or
> B) throwing money at the situation.

I've moved with both friends and professional movers helping me and every time it's been the same amount of anxiety. You don't realize the sheer amount of crap you have until you decide what's moving with you and then go through the motions of boxing it up, moving it into the van, moving it out of the van, moving it into the space, unboxing it, and then finding a place for it. It's enough to make you a minimalist, at least for a few weeks.

While I can't help you with the highly emotional trials of moving, here are some tips you can either use or disregard at your discretion. But hey, I've only moved seven awful times in Manhattan, what do I know?

GET RID OF AS MUCH STUFF AS HUMANLY POSSIBLE
While I distrust the Marie Kondo method of discarding items that don't "spark joy" when you hold them, if you can't picture yourself getting upset over never seeing it again, *sell or give it away*. Many charities will even physically come pick up your donations, so you can schedule a local favorite to swing by before the move.

RESEARCH MOVING COMPANIES
Your best bet is to go with a friend's recommendation because they've already dealt with them. But you should look at other choices, too. Price is obviously a big factor, but you should also look into their fine print, services, and refund and damage policies. Other factors to consider: Do they need to show a certificate of insurance to your building prior to moving you? Do they have something in the fine print about not having to move anything that's not properly boxed up? Does your building only allow you to move during certain windows of time during the day, and that company is already booked when you need to move? You'll be surprised at the disturbing number of factors that come into picking a moving company.

MAKE SURE YOUR UTILITIES WILL BE DISCONNECTED THE DAY OF
Unless you desperately need your WiFi (oh yeah, electricity too), you'll need to contact your internet, electricity, cable, and gas providers to let them know

you'll no longer be in that space. Don't put it off and let them know months after the fact. Conversely, hook up your utilities at your new place in advance.

CHANGE YOUR ADDRESS

The US postal service is gonna charge you a whole dollar to forward your mail, FYI. But this is a big one, especially if you have sensitive mail. Make sure your address is changed with your banks and credit cards as well.

BUY RENTERS INSURANCE AHEAD OF TIME

Oh, so you don't want to buy renters insurance? Hahahahahhahahahaha-hahahah—you're so screwed. Renters insurance covers your possessions and your ass if something bad happens to someone visiting you on your property. Some of the "luxury" buildings I've lived in (trust me, I was in the fake room portion) want you to insure up to an insane amount, but usually it won't cost you more than $150 for the year for peace of mind. Insurance covers everything from your laptop to your wardrobe in case anything goes wrong, and renters insurance usually covers most natural disasters and crime. On the latter note, take photos of your more important and expensive possessions so if they're stolen the insurance company can't argue that they never existed.

START PACKING EARLIER THAN YOU THINK YOU NEED TO

Life happens—you're required to go to a friend's birthday party, then you're hungover, then you have to stay late at work for a few nights...you get the drift. Make yourself a drink, put on a #tbt playlist, do whatever you need to do to start wrapping up your more valuable and delicate items ASAP.

USE PACKING TAPE

It ends poorly if you don't. Much like your ex, scotch or painter's tape will fail you. Every damn time.

WRAP YOUR DISHES AND OTHER BREAKABLES IN UNDERWEAR, SOCKS, AND OTHER LIGHTER GARMENTS

It's like a two-in-one! Otherwise, use bubble wrap, and stack your dishes vertically rather than horizontally.

USE WHATEVER STORAGE YOU OWN TO PACK THINGS IN

Those L.L. Bean "Boat and Totes"? Those seagrass baskets? Your laundry bin? Don't pack them, pack stuff in them.

TAKE PICTURES OF HOW YOUR ELECTRONICS AND OTHER PRECARIOUS ITEMS ARE SET UP

This will cut down on the "which cord goes to what" panicking.

PACK AN OVERNIGHT BAG AND CLEANING SUPPLIES BEFORE YOU MOVE

This way you'll have what you need for the night and the next morning, plus cleaning supplies for any weird things you encounter and need to get rid of immediately to feel comfortable in your new home.

IF YOU OWN A FRIDGE, DEFROST IT AT LEAST A DAY BEFORE YOU MOVE

First of all, good for you! Secondly, the last thing you want is a nasty fridge in your new space.

TAKE PHOTOS OF YOUR NEW APARTMENT BEFORE YOU MOVE IN (IF YOU'RE RENTING)

This way you can prove to the landlord that, for example, you didn't make those scuff marks, they were already there. For extra security, include a newspaper with that day's date on there in the photos. It'll be harder for them to argue with you later (my own landlord told me this).

LUXURY BUILDINGS VERSUS WALK-UPS

How you want to live as well as where is always an important question. Considering your existing salary and lifestyle, what can you afford? Equally as important, what can you tolerate?

As we've gone over, life is too short to live somewhere you hate, but at the same time you need to have enough money to live an active (okay, somewhat destructive) lifestyle while also saving and investing some of your hard-earned cash.

A walk-up will have much more bang for your buck in terms of square footage, but you'll be missing out on amenities. (And calling for maintenance whenever you damn well feel like it.) If you're the type of person who would prefer to stretch out and use your space for entertaining or having a pet, a walk-up may be the better option for you.

If you'd gladly switch out space for amenities, or can afford both space and amenities, then a luxury building might be for you!

Examples of amenities found in luxury buildings include:
Gardens, a doorman, elevator service, gym, pool, package room, lounges, office space, extra kitchen space, playgrounds, childcare, laundry rooms, spas, dry cleaning, maid service...the list can go on and on to the point where you feel like you're living in a hotel. But when you're shelling out easily three grand for a studio, it should sure as hell feel like it.

WALL ART—A NECESSITY

One of the caveats of being an adult is actually framing your art and not just tacking up posters willy-nilly like you're trying to get back at your parents for confiscating your Bud Light Lime.

The truth is your home will look scary as hell without anything on the walls. You don't want your place to look like somewhere you're just passing through as opposed to a safe, personalized space.

Find art you love, or can at least live with, and find appropriate frames. Frames can get expensive pretty quickly, so if you're not looking for the baroque floor-length one of your dreams then places like IKEA, Target, and Home Goods will suffice. Thrift shops will also have these in spades, and you can score super-cheap art you can scrap just to keep the frame.

If you're not a huge print or original art lover, there are other things you can hang in their stead:

FRAMED SCARVES

Love the print of your scarf but lament not wearing it as much as you like? Frame it and hang it. This is an especially nice touch if you've inherited some fancy silk scarves (like Hermès or other luxury designers), if you're not a scarf person and still want to show the accessory the respect it deserves.

VINTAGE MAGAZINES, COMIC BOOKS, OR ADS

Want to display some of the more fun elements of your magazine or comic book collection? It's a great way to impart some of your personality without spending extra on decor.

MORE ILLUSTRIOUS WALLPAPER

Whether you bought or are renting, there are so many cool wallpaper options out there if you want to make a big impact at lower cost. There are even wallpaper options that don't disturb the paint underneath if you're renting; you just peel them off before you move out.

HANGING ART

I suck at hanging art so I always bribe someone to do it for me with liquor. However, if you're more self-sufficient, I applaud you, and this is how you tackle it.

> "Why is there a makeshift putting green in your apartment? You don't even like golf."

> "If you build it, they will come."

- **When you have a stud**
  The most secure way to hang your art or racks or hooks is to find and drill it into a stud. Studs are pieces of wood located behind the drywall that make up the wall's frame. Use a stud finder to find the wood in your wall and use a power drill to slowly create a hole where you marked and measured. Now, attach your screw to the drill and drill it where you made the hole. Finally, hang your art and admire the tangibility of your domestic prowess.

- **When you don't have a stud**
  If there's no stud and you're hanging art straight into the drywall, there's a few ways you can go about it without pulling your hair out.

  - **Nails**
    You can hang your lighter artwork with nails. Just lightly hammer a nail where you want to hang your art, and voila! You're good to go. (This should work with most IKEA frames.)

  - **Anchor**
    Those weird see-through plastic screws are actually drywall anchors. You insert the anchor into the wall after you make your hole and before you insert the screw. This way, the anchor holds onto the screw and your art will be safe/not come crashing down in the middle of the night and give you a heart attack.

  - **Removable adhesive strips**
    If you're renting and not thrilled with the prospect of making holes in rental property you could get charged for, then double-sided adhesive strips or command hooks are the way to go. I've used these over the years and my only issue has been that if the strips are next to a heater, they come loose over time.

- **Patching up holes**
  So, what happens if you're renting and put holes in your walls? Something as small as nail holes to hang pictures usually won't affect your security deposit (especially if you're in a luxury building and they're going to charge you a repainting fee anyway), but if you're being paranoid and want to cover all your tracks, this should do the trick:

  Step 1: Remove the nail, preferably with the back of your hammer.

  Step 2: Take a tiny bit of spackle and fill the hole, wiping off any extra so the wall will be smooth.

  Step 3: Paint over it.

  Step 4: Blow your security deposit check on anything to get your mind off the fact you went through the hell of moving. Or reinvest in your next apartment.

> Had a dream that my building had a washer/dryer, if you want proof of how low the bar has been set.

INTERIOR DESIGN TIPS FOR SMALLER SPACES

Making the most of your somewhat cramped quarters is a valuable life skill, and one that many city dwellers have mastered over time. You can outsmart your apartment's lack of storage or square footage through certain tricks of the eye and vertical installations. Including:

ADD A FULL-BODY MIRROR, OR LARGER MIRRORS. OR MIRRORS ANYWHERE AND EVERYWHERE, REALLY.
It makes the space feel larger because of the reflection. Plus think of all the thirst-trap selfie opportunities.

CREATE SPACES FOR YOURSELF
Where you work, where you sleep, where you eat—in a perfect world they would all be separate from one another. However, life doesn't always work out that way and you have to make do. Even just placing chairs and dressers and TVs in certain spots to unofficially make "zones" helps immensely.

BUY FURNITURE THAT HAS DUAL PURPOSES
That couch? Make sure it's a sleeper sofa. Your ottoman? If it's hollow, it can serve as storage space, plus act as a spot for guests to sit or to place a tray while entertaining. Any extra space on your bookshelf? Use it to display any decor or bartending supplies. Versatility is key when you don't have a ton of space to work with.

MINIMALISM IS YOUR FRIEND
I hate to say it, but the fewer possessions you have to take up space (one large couch instead of a few armchairs, a table instead of multiple ottomans), will help the room look less cluttered and more spacious. Plus, furniture is freaking expensive and terrible to move.

EXPLOIT ANY VERTICAL SPACE
Floor-length curtains will make the room look larger than it is. Why get a shorter bookcase when you get a much taller one that will hold more? Add floating shelves to the walls for extra storage space. Use and abuse those walls, they won't hold a grudge.

RESALE VALUE OF CLOTHES AND OTHER ITEMS

Clothing trends come and go, electronics quickly become outdated in favor of the next better thing, and furniture can ostensibly last forever when taken care of properly. *There's no shame in selling your possessions when you're tired of them, or buying secondhand when you don't want to blow your paycheck on the new version.* It's a more sustainable practice for both the environment and your wallet, and half the fun of buying secondhand is the story behind it.

CLOTHING
So, you want to sell your clothing. Good for you! Too many of us have

Is there a term for forced minimalism because you have no clos-et or cabinet space left in your studio apartment?

become victims of instant gratification and are holding on to one too many ironic band tees or spring jackets with some sort of floral motif. As you grow (both physically and emotionally), your style and tastes will change. And your wardrobe should grow along with that.

Fast fashion doesn't have a good resale price because it's just that—quickly and cheaply made to suit the trend of the moment. It doesn't hold up well in the wash and no one particularly wants to pay for your H&M leggings once you're done with them. It's usually not worth attempting to sell your fast fashion to secondhand retailers because the cash you'll get is nil and dragging it all there will be far too much effort for what you'll get in return. Donate, or trash it if it's truly gone through the ringer.

If it's a mid-level or luxury-brand item in decent condition, then you can consider selling it either to a brick-and-mortar secondhand store or online communities like eBay, Poshmark, or TheRealReal. Once again, don't be shocked by how little you'll probably get for your item. The resale value of clothes isn't great, especially when retail isn't doing too hot to begin with and you can grab what you want on double clearance off the rack. But then again, money is money and every little bit helps. Or at least covers a round at happy hour.

If you're buying secondhand clothes, there a few things to take into account.

- What size are you in that specific brand and does it tend to shrink in the wash? Oftentimes you need to try on a secondhand item or see its measurements online. The person trying to unload it might be doing so because it's no longer their size after ignoring the "dry clean only" label.

- Can you return it? A lot of secondhand stores and sellers don't take returns so you really have to love it.

- What the hell is wrong with it? Check for holes, snags, and tears—someone might have sneakily dropped it off without warning a sales associate, or an associate might have missed a flaw while inspecting it. If you find an irregularity and still want the item, point out the issue and they'll usually take a percentage off the price of the garment. Sewing on that extra button (usually found on the interior cuff or a hem) might save you even more money than you anticipated.

- Take advantage of the Instagram effect—people getting rid of their

Dressing for warmer weather is always such a thot process.

special occasion and more elevated outfits after they wore it to a single event. No one wants to be consistently photographed in the same dress or super conspicuous outfit. More often than not, you can score a super nice cocktail or black tie option on eBay and other resale sites for the same cost as renting it. If you have the closet space, I'd go with the former.

ELECTRONICS

Some of our most valuable items are our laptops, phones, TVs, and the like. And with good reason—how else would we communicate, or you know, enjoy living?

A good rule of thumb when purchasing second-hand electronics is asking yourself how badly you need it/ how much it would screw up your life if it suddenly wasn't working. You can purchase refurbished electronics from the seller or a third party, but you might not know how good of a condition it's in until you're almost done with a presentation you have to deliver to the C-Suite tomorrow morning and it decides to implode.

I highly endorse selling your electronics when you're done with them. Worst case scenario, a third party company or entity will take your phone or laptop for parts (if it's a decent brand), or someone on Craigslist will cart away your old TV. You just might need to set the bar lower than what you initially thought you'd get for it.

FURNITURE

Dude, furniture is expensive. You don't realize how much it is to furnish an apartment or home until you're in the thick of it and come to the conclusion that you're going to blow the equivalent of a nice vacation on a couch—that you may not even like that much!!!

Do not grab mattresses and other seedy looking items like love seats off the street. They may have bed bugs, and fumigating your whole place will probably cost more than the item you grabbed. You may not be above snagging freebies, but you're above a vermin problem.

If you're buying secondhand furniture from a store or website, then you have much, much less to worry about. People no longer want furniture for a variety of reasons—they may not like it anymore, they don't want to move it, or it no longer goes with their apartment or decor. None of those reasons mean that there's something wrong with it for you.

THE ARGUMENT FOR CARRYING CASH

Cash, physical tender, dough—it's important to always have some on hand

"I made an unboxing vlog."

"That's just what you drunkenly picked up at Walgreens last night in addition to your prescriptions."

even as fewer and fewer people carry it. I suggest always having at least 20 bucks on you in case of tipping emergencies, or if your phone dies and you can't access any digital passes, subscriptions, or ride-hailing apps. You'll also thank yourself later when your credit or debit card statement isn't a bunch of $2 purchases that you should have just paid for with wadded up dollar bills, as the good lord intended. Plus, every time you use cash for a purchase is another instance you've successfully evaded identify theft!

Other less fun reasons for carrying a wad of bills in your wallet:

- Tolls
- Suspended credit cards
- Splitting bills

More fun reasons

- Tipping coat check and any hotel or building service workers
- Tinder for lighting cigars
- Something to throw at your significant other when they complain about your spending too much time at your job

FAKING YOUR WAY INTO PRIVATE RESTROOMS

This is more for urban areas, but if you're dressed somewhat nicely, you shouldn't have an issue confidently walking into a hotel or restaurant and heading straight to the bathroom. You've been in enough spaces to navigate your way to where the restrooms probably are—don't ask the concierge because that will arouse suspicion. Follow your gut and get the porcelain throne you deserve.

Fast casual and more grab-and-go restaurants have realized you might only be there for their convenient commode, and may have installed locks that only employees can open with a key, or can only be opened with the code you get with your receipt. You might need to pony up a few bucks for a soft drink but when you really have to go, it's more than worth it.

A more realistic definition of "fake it until you make it."

Other places with "decent" public restrooms include: malls, higher-end stores that cater to clientele that expect a restroom, and food courts of any kind.

HANGOVERS

There are, unfortunately, usually consequences for drinking. Even if you applaud your decisions in hindsight (who knew your high school crush was that easy?), your head is now splitting, you're nauseous, and every part of you, including your pride, hurts.

We've all been there, and we'll all be there time and time again unless you quit cold turkey. However, there are precautions you can take to mitigate the pain you'll feel the next morning—or all afternoon—depending on your tolerance and metabolism, which unfortunately, will begin to fail you in your mid- or late-twenties.

Ways to combat the inevitable hangover:

- **Have a glass of water after every drink.** This makes you more alert and nearly guarantees you not getting too hammered.

- **Pre-game with coconut water.** In college we all pulled the "I'm going to mix vodka with Gatorade and beat the system!" pre-game. Now that we're older, you can still certainly do that, but coconut water is a more socially acceptable alternative and mixes pretty well with rum. Another cool trick is making coconut water ice cubes so they slowly water down your drink.

Even if, despite all your valiant efforts, you still wake up feeling like death, here are a few things to check off before acknowledging that your day is more or less shot.

- **Physical exercise.** Who knew activity—rather than lying in the fetal position regretting everything you've said and done in the past 24

"No you cannot board your flight early because you 'feel it's best emotionally.' And can you stop openly doing shots in the waiting area?"

hours—was the number-one cure for a hangover? You'll sweat out the booze, your metabolism will kick into gear, you'll want to drink water; it's counterintuitive as hell, but it's scientifically proven.

- **An IV Drip**. Are you a doctor, a nurse, or are dating one? Consider an IV drip which will have you feeling human again in no time. There are also services that come to your home and administer the IV for you, but they're expensive. Apparently you can also order IV service poolside at some Vegas hotels, as I've gleaned from Instagram and friends that work in law or finance.

- **Getting high**. The most natural of cures, getting super high to numb the pain of existence will definitely help quell nausea and your headache. (Not recommended if you were actually planning on doing things that day or it's illegal in your state.)

- **Pedialyte and Gatorade, or hangover pills.** The ol' standbys are still here to help you through thick, thin, and your own personal hell. If I'm feeling especially terrible, I'll take hangover pill supplements and then wash them down with half a bottle of Pedialyte or as much Gatorade as I can possibly handle.

  What if you can't keep liquids down? When I'm irreconcilably hungover the idea of sucking down water makes me want to hug the porcelain throne. Gatorade and Pedialyte popsicles to the rescue. They come in flavors that won't make you gag, and if you keep them in your freezer, they're pretty good to suck on in the morning while you're lying in bed with your self-loathing. You can buy Pedialyte popsicles but I tend to make my own Gatorade ones to save some cash.

Another way to combat the hell you willingly put yourself through is the hair of the dog that bit you. *This is not a cure, and not recommended because it could turn into a cyclical pattern of alcohol abuse.* But, if you already had brunch plans, this isn't the worst idea. You'll perk up because the booze will mask some of the discomfort you're feeling and force you to be more lively.

Shockingly, it's even backed up by science. Methanol is found in alcohol, and it's converted to formaldehyde in the body. By drinking ethanol (more liquor) it can stop this conversion and you just piss out the toxins. Ah, the magic of even more terrible decisions.

If you don't have brunch plans and there's no way in Hell you're leaving the sanctity of your home, here's two foolproof options that'll help haul you back on your ass.

- **Bloody Mary**
  There are a million variations of this beloved breakfast drink, but here are the basic ingredients that you can tailor to your wants, needs,

¼ cup of tomato juice A jigger and a half of vodka (or mezcal if you want a Bloody Maria, I love the Montelobos brand) ¼ teaspoon lemon juice	1 teaspoon of Worcestershire sauce ¾ teaspoons of horseradish Three dashes of hot sauce Salt and pepper to taste
Stir together and add pickles, lemons, celery, old bay, olives, cocktail onions—literally anything you want that will both taste good and look decent enough to go on Instagram.	

desires, and dreams. You can also just buy Bloody Mary mix and dump in as much vodka or mezcal as necessary.

- **Vodka and Pickle Juice**
Another hangover "cure" is pickle juice, and I don't swear by it, but will reach for it if I'm in enough pain. It does supposedly help with muscle cramps and is extremely salty and packed with electrolytes. Adding liquor helps quell the pain even more, and I add two parts vodka to one part pickle juice, but you can just as easily do this with whiskey for a bastardized pickleback.

CHAPTER 2

Etiquette

Things are great in the Bell Jar!

Etiquette in the digital age has become a less defined and more constantly evolving concept. If you're questioning what to do or say within the often blurred lines of a social or professional situation, it's not due to your utter lack of decorum—we're in novel territory and most of us are guilty of sometimes missing the boat.

Rather than continue to grasp at sea-turtle-killing straws, let's address some of the old, the new, and the "I'm not sure what the hell is really going on, but let's roll with it" etiquette guidelines.

Etiquette Essentials

For a story I was reporting, I was lucky enough to attend etiquette courses at the Plaza Hotel with Myka Meier, founder of Beaumont Etiquette, and the whole experience was a lot less stuffy than it sounds. Myka is awesome and explained that etiquette is about instilling confidence, so you don't have to worry at events about the background noise that is your social anxiety telling you everything you do is wrong. *The purpose of a gathering is to concentrate on the people you're with, not panicking about your subpar social graces.*

The concept of proper etiquette may seem antiquated and could be confused with snobbery, but it's always been about thoughtfulness. For example, extra cutlery at a dinner setting may look pretentious but it's there so you, the guest, can have everything you will possibly need.

Some basic pointers I learned during class:

MEETING

- Modern etiquette dictates that handshakes are gender neutral, and both parties are expected to stand.

- When in doubt, give someone a handshake versus a hug or air or cheek kiss. Handshakes go right hand to right hand, and there's a big difference between an assertive and aggressive handshake.

- Every minute you're late, give the person you're meeting two minutes of advance notice. For example if you're running ten minutes late, let them know twenty minutes beforehand.

- Don't apologize profusely if you're late; if you make it a big deal it becomes a big deal.

- Do not talk about money, sex, politics, or vices like drinking and smoking in polite company. Basically, know your audience.

- Don't ask what the person does for a living as the first question, it seems opportunistic.

- Show up ten minutes early to a business meeting, ten minutes after the start time to a party in a home, and right on time for a networking event.

DINING

- Never put your elbows on the table, regardless of whether it's a business or formal dining situation. You can rest your forearms on the table.

- If you're unable to check your jacket, fold it in half and place it either over the back of your chair or across the banquette (the longer seat against the wall that isn't a chair).

- Your fork is always in the left hand, the knife in the right. "Fork" and "left" also happen to have the same number of letters, as do "knife" and "right."

- When placing your napkin in your lap, make sure the crease is always facing you.

- When wiping your mouth, bring the napkin up to your mouth and dab using the interior of the folded napkin before placing it back in your lap.

"Please stop using the silver fish forks with the Red Lobster takeout—4/20 is not good enough of a holiday excuse."

Don't be a shellfish prick

By using the interior you're protecting your bottoms from food stains.

- The napkin in your chair is a sign to service staff that you're coming back.

- Don't announce that you're going to the men's or ladies' room, just say "excuse me." No one wants to envision what you do when you leave their company.

- Pinch and place the napkin to the left of your plate as a signal to the service staff when you're done with the meal.

- When holding a wine glass with a stem, actually hold it at the stem. It's there so your body temperature doesn't heat up the chilled wine.

GIVING TOASTS

We've all heard bad toasts, and those are the ones that go down in the annals of memory. The long-winded drunken tangents, the panicked looks around the room when the speaker makes it more of a roast than a tribute, the grandparents swiftly exiting the room as a college friend brings up the betrothed's storied, highly adventurous past (involving most of a lacrosse team and a chicken coop).

That being said, toasts are hard! You're supposed to deliver a witty and funny monologue that's sentimental without getting soppy. You also have to tailor the content and tonality to the audience at hand, and put on a good show while simultaneously not making it about you. And all the while, keeping it short and sweet.

AT YOUR FORMER SORORITY SISTER'S WEDDING: "Cathy always dressed like a slutty soccer mom, but I guess dress for the job you want, right?"*crickets*

On the bright side, everyone is already rooting for you because you were clearly important enough to the person or couple being honored that they asked you to speak about them. Plus, lest we forget, this really isn't about you.

If you're making a wedding toast, first of all, introduce yourself and your connection to the bride or groom. Promise that you'll keep it short (and do so) and share a funny anecdote or two that speaks to their good qualities, or their devotion to the person they just said "I do" to. Finally, speak to the future and the happiness that will surely follow the bride and groom. Any and all jokes about how long you assume this will last should not make it into the speech, even if all the guests are silently thinking it.

If you're giving a business-related toast, keep it short and speak to the past, present, and future. Example: "Never forget when so-and-so joined the company, they're making great strides, and I look forward to seeing what they do on their next venture." Feel free to share an anecdote about their stellar work or character traits, but remember this is far less sentimental than a wedding toast (thank God).

TIPS FROM THE MODERN GENTLEMAN (who literally wrote the book on manners)
David Coggins, man about town and *NYT* bestselling author, offers some of his own personal etiquette tips for the younger set.

- Never walk into a restaurant—or any room for that matter—while on the phone.
- When arriving at a party, always bring something, even if the host says bring nothing.
- Don't split a bill more than two ways.
- No saving seats in crowded bars.
- "Work emergency" is an excuse to be used sparingly.
- Don't text that you're five minutes away unless you're five minutes away.
- You already know you're on your phone too much.

HOST GIFTS

We've all been in the situation where we'd rather crash with a friend than shell out hundreds of dollars a night for a hotel room. In college we were happy with a bunch of pillows, a blanket, and a floor, but now that we're older it's likely you'll be offered a guest bedroom. Or if you're staying in NYC or SF, you'll be lucky if they have a couch. I, for one, really miss having a couch.

"Look, I got you some gift certificates."

"That's a blank prescription pad you stole from your ex."

As a token of your gratitude, goodwill, and friendship, you should bring a gift in exchange for their time and their tailoring their schedule to your needs. If you've ever hosted someone before you know it's a huge time and energy suck, even if you truly love the guest and look forward to them staying with you.

There are different levels of host gifts and what you bring depends on whom you're staying with and for how long.

For a quick visit, like a dinner or party:

CANDLES
"Nicer candles are so cathartic because you're literally setting money on fire."

They're great for re-gifting or using them yourself in your (literal) darkest hours. I tend to buy the ones I know I love when they go on sale, and store them either for my personal use or quick host gifts.

WINE, CHAMPAGNE, OR BOOZE
Bring wine for everything from parties to one-on-one friend times when you know you're inevitably going to end up drinking a glass (or several) on the couch. Champagne is for more celebratory events, like birthdays and divorces.

FLOWERS
"More than anything, I thought you'd appreciate the phallic vase."

Only monsters don't appreciate flowers, and they're hard to screw up. Unless you bring carnations; carnations are trash flowers and you should know better than that.

If you want to bring something that's both beautiful and effortless on your part, grocery stores like Trader Joe's and Whole Foods offer exquisite, pre-

Whine Pairings

"A sommelier but instead of pairing wine with food, they recommend pairings for small injustices."

arranged bouquets for under $10. If your host has a more trendy aesthetic, shade plants or succulents that are hard to kill (as discussed earlier) are also a safe bet.

Extended stays

If you're staying with someone for a few days, then it's better to bring a few things that they would appreciate, like nice barware or chic kitchen accessories, in addition to wine or liquor.

This is where stocking up on cool home items when they go on sale is a good idea. I'll raid sample sales for this explicit purpose, so this way I'm not caught off-guard and don't end up spending a ton on something meh whenever I need a quick turnaround on a host gift. Ideally it should have a gift receipt so they can promptly return it if they secretly hate it.

"For someone who rarely makes anything other than vodka sodas, you have a disturbingly well stocked bar tools collection."

Paying for dinners out, or buying groceries and cooking (if they're cool with your using their kitchen), are also an excellent idea, but only if you're competent. Your ability to make a keg out of a watermelon doesn't count in the culinary skills department.

Home is where the WIFI is.

IF YOU'RE CRASHING AT A FRIEND'S PLACE IN-BETWEEN APARTMENTS

Throw them rent money. Staying somewhere for weeks on end warrants cash; life is too short to piss off your good friends. If they insist that you're staying for free because you need somewhere to collect yourself and get back on your feet (we've all been there and it's not a fun place to be), then offer to at least go grocery shopping and make meals.

If you're staying in an empty apartment because the person is either away or on business, then make sure they walk into a clean apartment with a gift waiting for them upon their return.

THANK YOU NOTES

When you were younger, you likely had a family member breathing down your neck about writing thank you notes for birthday and holiday gifts. Now that you're older, you still have to force yourself to sit down and pen that thoughtful note, but in addition to writing them for gifts you receive, you should write a note whenever someone hosts you for a weekend or throws a more lavish party than a kegger.

Interview thank you notes are also a must, but given the speed of technology these days, an email should suffice, unless you drop it in the mail *as soon as the interview is over* or hand-deliver to the office if you're really itching to be noticed for the job.

I admit I'm not the best in the thank you note department outside of job interviews, and was floored when a friend sent me one for hosting her (on personalized stationary no less!). It makes a noticeable difference, and you can easily order your own, that ranges from extremely affordable templates to letterpress options. If you're stumped on where to start, Terrapin Stationers has a range of fun options with personality.

You most likely know how to pen a thoughtful thank you note, but make sure you express genuine gratitude by putting the attention on them (use "you" in the first line), specific examples of why you are appreciative, why you benefited from their generosity or expertise, and then thank them in the last line. Ta-da! You just went up several notches in someone's estimations.

TALKING ABOUT SALARIES $

It's generally considered rude to talk about how much money you make because you'll inevitably cause an uncomfortable rift when the rest of the group either makes more or less than the proffered number.

Off-the-cuff jokes about how you're paid badly is an inoffensive standby, but ostentatiously flaunting your wealth is tacky as hell and won't gain you any friends—except the gold-digging kind.

> NOTE: It's generally a good (if not great) idea to discuss salaries with other people in your field. We all need to be more transparent about our incomes, especially with coworkers and colleagues who aren't getting their fair share. Late-stage capitalism is a cruel beast, and we need to fight back wherever and whenever we can.

SPLITTING BILLS WITH FRIENDS

The all-too-common nightmare scenario: you're at a birthday dinner and rather than divvy up the bill according to who chose what, the asshat who ordered the steak and enough whiskey to incapacitate a small gorilla suggests you all split it evenly.

If you're the one who didn't drink and got a small salad to save money, it's enough to deter you from eating out with groups altogether. The important thing is to not have an issue speaking up when such situations arise, or go in with a pre-planned method of attack.

Don't forget to send a thank you note to your dad for doing your taxes!

As a "coastal elite" I feel like I'm missing out on a lot of the "coastal" and "elite" stuff.

"Trust the process" doesn't apply to scoring decent brunch reservations.

THERE ARE A FEW WAYS SPLITTING BILLS CAN GO:

YOU ALL SPLIT THE BILL

Usually it's easiest and best practice for everyone to split the bill, and if someone got a glass of wine or an extra appetizer, they'll leave the tip.

YOU SPEAK UP, EITHER FOR YOU OR A FRIEND

If this is going to be a hefty bill and you ordered something on the cheaper side, speak the hell up. Say something along the lines of, "Hey, I'm on a budget and ordered XYZ for that reason, can I just Venmo you?" and that should take care of it. Everyone has a budget in some way, shape, or form and they can't expect you to blow through yours out of politeness.

Similarly, if your friend didn't order something expensive and there's a motion to split, say they should only leave the tip or Venmo someone. Your friend will be eternally grateful that you brought it up and will return the favor down the line.

ONE PERSON COVERS IT

Everyone Venmos or digitally sends money to one person who picks up the whole tab. This way, everyone can send their individualized amounts, and hopefully the person who's throwing down their card doesn't get screwed over. This is also exponentially easier on your server and they'll be grateful for it.

ASK FOR YOUR OWN CHECK AHEAD OF TIME

If you're truly that worried about your friends' spending habits, call ahead to the restaurant and ask for your own check, or pull the waiter aside and discreetly ask them. This way, two checks will arrive and you can just take care of your own. If you're worried about looking cheap, say you were drinking at the bar earlier and just asked them to move your tab over to the table.

This trick can also be used if your friend or S.O. always insists on picking up the check (a good problem to have) and you want to treat them without fighting tooth and nail over the bill. Call ahead and say you're picking up the check, or give the restaurant your credit card in the beginning and explain you're taking care of it.

TEXT ETIQUETTE

Humans are communicative by nature. We let each other know when we're happy, sad, miss them, or are a few drinks deep past midnight and on our way over in an Uber. The issue with always putting it in writing is that you can't gauge sarcasm, mood, and tonality from a smattering of words hastily punched onto a screen.

The best you can do is consider your audience whenever you're texting with them, and converse in a way they're comfortable with. Whether that's the Queen's English, emojis, memes, or nudes, is your burden and data plan to bear.

A few things to keep in mind:

Use full sentences with older folks
Unless they're intent on being the "cool mom" and already know all the abbreviations, lmao.

Turn off your notification sounds
We get it, you have friends. We don't need to hear dinging or see a light every millisecond because of the group chat.

Never text "k" as a response
"K" is the universal letter that insinuates you're mad or tired of the recipient's inane stories. Be the better person and give them the extra letter of instant gratification. Add the O, it may be one of the few times you can deliver it anyway.

Prevent yourself from intentionally waiting days to text back
Yes, even if the other party is doing it to you. The person you're talking to is either playing head games, honestly forgetful, or trying to send a message. If it's the latter, they should hopefully be more upfront with you, but actions speak louder than words.

Turn off your text previews
You don't know when someone else will be glancing at your phone. You don't want them to see snippets of your more intimate conversations.

Don't send explicit photos unless they're asked for
You never know how many people and group chats will get access to your pics. Make sure you know the person super well before you send anything.

Always replying with emojis makes you look like an idiot

"Self-care Sunday!!!!" she yelled at her cat. The cat licked its paw and silently wished that Brad would text back too.

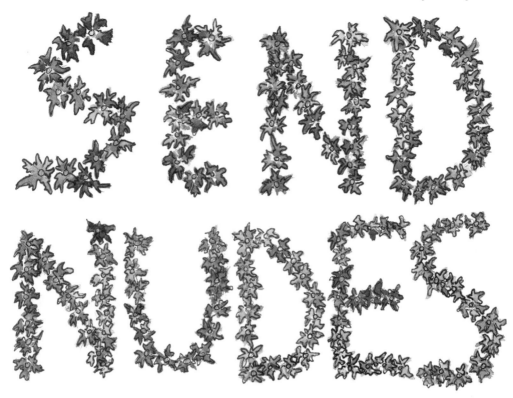

"I got you flowers"

My favorite way to start a sentence is, "First of all, how dare you."

Expressing real, layered, and varied emotions through words is a valuable skill. It may be easier for you to escape the gravity of certain conversations by letting your answers be loosely interpreted with a string of cartoon martini glasses and pills, but that's no way to go through life.

Reply in a similar manner

If they wrote two words, don't respond with a novel. Also give them a chance to answer—a text conversation requires at least two people. Don't double or triple text unless you know them or need to get relevant, timely info across. A ton of unprompted texting without any reciprocity will make you look batshit crazy. I should know!

Know when to end the conversation

If the paragraphs won't stop coming or both of you are too polite to end the conversation, either just stop responding at a neutral point or say you're going to bed or are in a meeting. Chances are the other party will be grateful you're signing off too.

REGIFTING

When you've received a lovely gift that isn't exactly "you," there's always the option to regift it. I don't mind regifting in theory because when I like a quality item, its origins aren't grounds for declining it. Because my opinion on regifting is very much on the more apathetic side, I turned to Myka Meier again for her more qualified thoughts on the matter.

> # The best birth control I can think of is not being able to eat sushi or drink coffee or wine for nine months.

"Regifting is dangerous etiquette territory, so proceed with caution! If regifting is ever discovered, it could cause the person who gave it to you to be offended and hurt, and if there is even the slightest chance someone could find out you refitted their present to you, avoid doing it. If you do decide to regift an item, because, for instance, you received a duplicate gift and you know someone who would love it, make sure it's in its original packaging, has never been used (no, not even once!), and is not personalized in any way. When else should you not regift? If something was made specially for you or was chosen with such thought that it was obviously for you. Never regift in the same friend or family circle—you don't want Aunt Edith recognizing the oddly familiar picture frame sitting on your sister's counter."

PREGNANCY

There's nothing more alarming than the first friend that gets pregnant on purpose. The alarm fades into happiness. Then more panic. And then, happiness again. Kids are a big, big deal and your friend is going to want and need your support.

Be congratulatory, and mentally prepare yourself for this new, vicariously-lived chapter of your life, perhaps arriving before you wanted it to happen.

BABY SHOWERS

Right after you shelled out for a wedding present, they had the audacity to go and get knocked up and you're stuck buying a baby shower gift. (JK, JK, kids are adorable.)

"Life isn't measured by the breaths we take, but the moments that take your breath away."

"Can you just prescribe me my fucking asthma meds?"

If it's a coworker or an acquaintance, a $25 gift will suffice. Spring for $50 for friends and $100+ for best friends and family.

If the person or couple doesn't have a baby registry, then diapers or assorted toys and baby essentials should work. Usually if it's an office baby shower they'll just pass around a card with a suggested donation and you can give what you can/want/deem appropriate if they've been passive-aggressively ignoring your work emails.

TOUCHING OF THE STOMACH/INVASIVE QUESTIONS

No one likes their stomach being pointed out, let alone touched. People usually don't like sharing overly personal things, like their intimate discomforts and anything potentially graphic in nature. No matter how curious you are about their physical state, err on the side of leaving the tired woman be.

GIVE THEM YOUR DAMN SEAT

Pregnant women are growing another human life in their body and it is literally sucking the life force out of them. They're probably tired and will happily accept your bus/subway seat, and if they don't want it, will wave you off. But hey, you tried and it's the thought that counts.

DID THEY GAIN A LOT OF WEIGHT OR ARE THEY PREGNANT?

Dude, don't ask. They could be post-pregnancy and haven't lost the weight yet and you bringing it up will make them feel terrible. Also if they're in the process of popping out a kid and want you to be aware of that fact, they'll let you know.

DEATH

Dealing with death sucks in every way, shape, and form, and everyone has their own personal coping mechanisms. That's why it's best to deliver your condolences and not be offended if your sentiments aren't noted or thanked by the griever.

Grappling with the death of someone who you didn't know but was close to a friend, coworker, or family member can be awkward because you never really know what to say. The situation just sucks and no amount of "I'm so sorry for your loss" will make it better. Just let them know you're always there if they need someone to talk to or just hang out with, and don't shy away from asking them to hang out and do the things you would usually do together to give them some sense of normalcy.

My friend Katrina Masterson recently dealt with the loss of her mom, and offered this advice to friends of the bereaved who want to know what to say or do: "My friends were a big part in helping me when my mother was sick. Calling me up to make sure I had eaten that day, or just letting me know they were close by if I needed to step out for a drink, were the little things that got me through it all. It's always comforting to know someone is there to listen to your problems, and to just be there for you. I appreciated that they would make everything about me, but I found asking them what was happening in their world was a great way to get my mind off things, even for a moment. Being filled in on social gossip I had missed out on also provided some much-needed comic relief. Hearing something as trivial as Becky's drunken antics at a party is sometimes more hilarious when you're going through something intense."

FUNERALS

Funerals are all very different and vary by religion and culture. Open casket, closed casket, graveside service, sitting shiva...there are a million different variations that ultimately come down to the family's choice. If you're going to a service that then goes to a cemetery, only go graveside if you're close with the family or the deceased.

If you're going to the deceased's family's home, bring flowers or something edible that won't go bad too quickly. If the family cites that they want donations in the deceased's name to the charity of their choice in lieu of sending flowers (as is customary in the Jewish religion), then abide by their wishes and do so.

You don't have to necessarily wear black—gray and understated, dark tones are also acceptable but make sure it's not flashy or anything less than tasteful. I've heard stories about mourners showing up to funerals in black bandage dresses; this is not the time or place for club wear, even if it's the only black clothes you can scrounge up.

Sharing a fond memory of the deceased to the bereaved is encouraged, but if you don't know what to say then, "My condolences to you and your family," is the safest.

Do not:
- Provide commentary, colorful or not, about how the person died. Car sex has taken too many good people from us, but we don't need to broadcast that.

Would love to get trained in martial arts because I bet ninjas are GREAT at avoiding old acquaintances.

- If the person died from illness, don't go over how it could have been prevented or other experimental surgeries or meds they could have tried.

- Tell the bereaved that you know how they feel—you don't. It comes off as rude, and this day is not about you.

- Act thrilled to see people, even if it's extended family you only get to see at weddings and funerals.

- Post to social media. Funeral selfies are not, and will never be, a thing.

IRISH OR FRENCH EXITING

Irish exiting, or leaving without saying goodbye to the host or other partygoers, is often a preferable option if there are A) a large number of people at the party, B) there's alcohol involved, or C) you came alone.

You may feel like it's rude, but let's be honest, very few people will care that you left. This isn't an attack on your friendships, people are usually preoccupied with their own affairs and your personal schedule is the least of their concerns. Instead, you can rest easy (preferably in bed with takeout and Netflix) rather than stand around for another 20 minutes, counting down the seconds until you can hit the pizza shop or take off your heels.

If the host is tasked with saying goodbye to every single person at the party, a huge chunk of time is going to be sucked into idle pleasantries neither of you care about. It's almost akin to wanting a medal for showing up.

If the host isn't surrounded by a big crowd, then by all means, say goodbye and that you had a great time, but if they're otherwise occupied then shoot them a thank you text the next day saying how great the party was. The host will probably appreciate the latter a lot more.

If it was a networking function, send a thank you email to the host if you want to follow up with them anyway for other professional reasons.

TIPPING

Ah yes, the constantly questioned etiquette behind tipping. When to do it, how much, and how often is often a moral and financial dilemma. Livelihoods often depend on tips, and your plunking down an additional 15-20% is a non-

Aren't happy hours just self-medication as a team building exercise?

negotiable even if you're completely broke. In some countries, it's rude to tip, and in some restaurants it's already thoughtfully accounted for in the bill. One of my favorite restaurants in NYC, Gramercy Tavern, already has the tip included with the meal and drink prices, and not exerting myself to do the math just adds to the elevated experience (I can't stress enough how much I hate math).

The general consensus is to tip a dollar a drink if you're paying by the round, or all lumped together at the end if you forked over your card and kept it open. If they're labor-intensive mixed drinks then tip 20% of what the drink cost.

If you're deadass broke and not enthusiastic about the idea of handing over extra cash in addition to a bar tab, don't go out. Our generation is notorious for drinking in our apartments or homes because A) we're in debt, and B) we realized how expensive it is to go out. Tipping is part of the night's expenses and should be factored into your budget.

If you had a shitty experience at a restaurant or bar then tip a little less than the normal amount, but remember that you're screwing over the wait staff and whomever they're pooling their money with. If it's a larger issue, calmly discuss it with the manager and don't take it out on the server.

If you're a regular at a restaurant or bar, then tip more than you usually would so the staff notices and you can become friendlier with them. Having a neighborhood bar or restaurant where you know the staff is often one of the better parts of adulthood. If it gets to the point where you're a welcome regular that's granted complimentary food or drinks, then tip on what the full bill would have cost with the comped items included.

HOLIDAY TIPPING

Holiday tipping can get grating if you're using a lot of services, but if you're already tipping regularly, then you can forgo the holiday tip.

If you live in a doorman building, then handing over a check or $100 bill (in an envelope) is standard practice around the holidays. In the past, I would hand over mine and my roommate's to whomever was in charge and they would all split it amongst themselves. I also recommend tipping anyone who gave you special care and attention, like the package room handler if they always take care to save things for you or call when something time-sensitive arrives.

Other people you should be tipping for the holidays, if you see them regularly:

- Personal trainer
- Salon staff
- Teacher
- Pet groomer
- Dog walker

If you're on a tighter budget, consider giving them homemade goods like cookies and a thoughtful note instead of cash or a check.

HOSPITAL VISIT ETIQUETTE

Hospital visits are never fun. It's terrifying to see a family or friend incapacitated, and there isn't much you can do besides spending time with them during visiting hours (if they're up for it) and bringing presents that can help take their mind off their current situation.

My friend and longtime wingman, Shane Duggan, recently had an unexpected ER visit, and while he told me that the flowers and cookies I brought him were lovely, he appreciated other gifts more:

"When I got home from the hospital, my friends surprised me with Seamless and Uber gift certificates, which were incredibly thoughtful and came in handy during my recovery. As pretty as they may be, you can't eat flowers and a casserole won't give you a ride to your doctor's appointment."

In hindsight, I should have got him gift certificates, but I'm still a fan of flowers.

The cool thing about mortality is at some point you won't have to make small talk with people you graduated from high school with.

UMBRELLA ETIQUETTE

One of my biggest grievances with New York is that, when it's raining, the sidewalk is like a giant, sopping-wet battleground. People barrel past you with enormous, dripping tents, trying to get to their next meeting, their eyes glued to their phone, knocking over whomever is in their path. I'm even mad at the hot Midtown guys in suits on those days. Here's how to not be that person:

"Not thrilled about the weather but at least I get to break out the hardy British countryside aesthetic," she said to the blank walls of her cubicle.

- Don't open your umbrella until you're outdoors. Screw bad luck, it's bad form.
- If you're passing someone that's shorter than you, raise your umbrella and let them pass.
- If you're the same height as the person you're passing, the person with the larger umbrella should raise it and let the other pass.
- As soon as you enter an indoor space, place your umbrella in the allotted bin or take a plastic bag so it doesn't drip everywhere.

BREAKING PLANS

Option 1: Don't make them at all!
As you get older you feel more and more gung ho about saying no to events, activities, and get-togethers because you realize how valuable your time is and that where you put your energy affects other parts of your life.

Tim Herrera, "Smarter Living" editor for *The New York Times*, offered some wise words on the art of saying "no." (We won't mention that hanging out with me while being the editor of a vertical called "Smarter Living" is the biggest self-own.)

"Humans are naturally social creatures. We crave interaction with others, and doing anything to upset that order can drive us mad with anxiety. (How many times have you laid in bed ruminating on a harmless-but-awkward thing you said to a coworker?)

So when we decline an opportunity—at work, in our personal life, wherever—it gives us the sense that we're breaking that implicit social contract. It feels confrontational, no matter how low the stakes.

Are notes from your therapist the new hall pass?

But all of those casual yeses we dole out add up! They leave us overcommitted to things we don't truly care about, sometimes meaning we don't have time to do the things we actually care about.

That's why you should say no, unapologetically and relentlessly.

If an opportunity inspires genuine excitement in you, and it aligns with your core and ambitions, go for it and give it everything you have. But anything short of that spark of excitement? It's a no.

This binary outlook—sure, a little over-the-top—will force you to figure out what's core to you. Once you're there, you'll know when a chance at work or personally affirms your identity, and saying no will feel easier than ever. Social contracts be damned."

Option 2: Cancel as far ahead as you possibly can
If there's a timing conflict (or let's be real, you get a better offer), let them know as far ahead as you possibly can and reschedule with date options if you actually want to see them. None of that, "Oh, let's get a drink sometime" BS we're all guilty of.

If you're bailing on a company event or something less personal, make sure to contact the event organizer or person who invited you as soon as you know you can't make it, so they can fill your spot.

Option 3: Make a valid excuse and don't provide too many details
Be honest whenever humanly possible, but when all else fails, blame health or work. But you can't do this that often or you'll get a reputation of someone who bails all the time, and no one wants to hang out with those types of people.

Caveats:
Once you bail, **do not post on social media** during the time you were supposed to be seeing them. The person you bailed on will most likely see it and feel like absolute crap.

If it's a dinner or something that was already paid for, you can't cancel unless you're actually ill, it's a business emergency, or someone had the audacity to go and die and have their funeral at the same time as Becky's engagement party. Becky should forgive you.

SOCIAL MEDIA

Social media etiquette is its own animal. I try to abide by the age-old rule: if you're questioning the post, don't upload it. While everyone has their own opinions about what is and isn't appropriate, you can only benefit from social media by using your own judgment and discretion. Ask yourself if you have something to lose (either personally or professionally) by posting certain things.

"What does she do for work?"

"She's an Instagram influencer with a slutty-Moonrise Kingdom Kingdom aesthetic."

Note: Even if you have a locked account, people are exceptionally screenshot happy. Never forget that little tidbit.

Aside from your own inherent rules regarding social media, here a few that I (attempt to) stand by.

DON'T OVERSHARE

No one wants to know every frigging detail of your day. Your family may love you unconditionally, but your followers are always more than happy to weed you out and clean up their timeline if you post too much. Oversharing not only reveals too much about your hopes, dreams, and fears to an unlimited number of people that don't really care about you, *but it's annoying as hell.*

Only post when you find something funny, amusing, and cool that's authentic and relevant to you or your friends/audience. That's how you stay interesting, thoughtful, and someone worth following.

DON'T BRAG

There's a fine line between tastefully showing off where you are and what you're doing and hitting people over the head with it. I personally follow editors and tastemakers because I know they're going to be in cooler places than I am, and by seeing the far better things they're doing I'm supposedly expanding my worldview. Hell yeah I want to see fancy restaurants in Italy and what's going on in a private jet—who knows if I'll ever get to experience it.

However, blatantly touting luxury items, vacations, or your significant other isn't going to gain you any friends. Who cares if you got a bunch of followers for posting over-the-top photos and videos if your friends secretly hate you for it?

DON'T GET TOO EMO

As a former emo kid, I know it's tempting to post song lyrics and melodramatic posts about the depressing state of the world and your place in it. But people are going to assume it's a cry for help, or that you're a sad sack who desperately needs a lifestyle makeover. Both are not ideal situations. Save the depressing content for Tumblr, a lovely hotbed for niche followings if there ever was one.

DON'T TAG PEOPLE IN UNFLATTERING PHOTOS

Tag unto others as you would have them tag unto you. In short, think of other people's emotions while tagging. You know how upset you would be if someone uploaded a terrible photo of you and had the audacity to link it to your social accounts.

BETTER YET, DON'T UPLOAD THE PICTURES AT ALL IF YOUR FRIEND LOOKS TERRIBLE

Be the better person. If you really, really want to post it because you look great in the photo or it's one of the few group shots you have, use your best judgment.

DON'T POST PHOTOS OF YOUR FRIENDS' KIDS WITHOUT THEIR PERMISSION

Thanks to A.I. technology and well, internet companies selling our personal data, some parents may be wary of splashing their kids' faces across the interwebs. That's their decision to make and not yours; always ask if it's alright to post a photo of their kids before you do it.

IGNORE THE TROLLS

For every wonderful interaction online there's usually some troll yelling about it and linking it to politics. Trolls are usually anonymous for a reason, and how big of a loser are they for spending their precious time making fun of strangers they'll never meet or see? Don't engage—block and ignore them, they're not worth your energy.

DON'T OVERLOAD YOUR FEEDS

Posting a ton of content at once is a stellar way for people to unfollow you. You should be posting to Instagram twice a day, max. Anything more and it gets obnoxious.

THIRST TRAPS

Posting thirst traps is so commonplace that it's become generally accepted (unless, as I've mentioned multiple times, this is a professional and straitlaced account).

Nonchalantly showing off your body to garner likes and comments is a fairly harmless ego boost—and an exercise in knowing your limits. Post them sparingly or your entire account will be the

"How do we know each other again?"

"You were hammered and kept yelling at the DJ to play the *Cruel Intentions* soundtrack."

equivalent of a thot catalog. And no one wants to be closely associated with a notorious thot or fuckboy, unless they're personally getting something out of it.

ARGUING WITH SOMEONE IN THE COMMENTS OF THEIR POST

There are only a few reasons why you should leave an unpleasant or provoking comment on someone's post.

- **If they stole your IP (intellectual property) or imagery or one of your friends' IP.** Meme accounts have no shame when it comes to stealing other people's content; if you see yours or a friend's without credit, feel free to shame them in the comments.

- **If they're posting something nasty about you, a friend, or family member.** How dare they? Feel free to defend the person they're attacking, but remember that you need to come off looking like the better, more mentally stable person.

- **If they posted a slur or something insensitive about someone's physical qualities.** That's just rude and shameful. Feel free to let them know.

FORGOT SOMEONE'S NAME?

I'm guilty of immediately forgetting peoples' names. It's a curse, one I wouldn't wish on most people (except my enemies, definitely my enemies).

The easiest and quickest way to get someone to say their name again is to introduce them to a friend who's nearby, so they think you're just being friendly and no one's the wiser. Saying their name to yourself three times upon introduction and using their name in a sentence right after meeting them helps immensely.

If none of those are working, ask someone else for their name when the person is out of earshot, or apologize and ask them for it again. Usually they won't be offended, unless this is the sixth time you've been introduced and they're getting fed up with your mental slip-ups.

AIRPLANE ETIQUETTE

Flying used to be an event that people dressed up for, sporting some of their finest duds and acting like they were going on a grand adventure. Now that the allure of air travel has mostly worn off, it's more like a free-for-all in both dress and demeanor as soon as you hit the security line. I'm not above throwing on leggings or a chic tracksuit (I did come of age in the Juicy Couture heyday), but bear in mind that you're more likely to be upgraded if you're dressed nicely and are polite.

DON'T BRING HOT FOOD ON THE PLANE

No one wants to smell the tantalizing aroma of a Shake Shack burger and fries or the fish sandwich you sadistically bought. Some people are already

"Stop asking if those airplane-shaped pins mean they successfully entered the Mile High Club."

feeling angsty or queasy, don't subject them to food they can't have or it will make them feel additionally ill when they're already not thrilled about flying.

DON'T HOG THE ARM REST
Feel out the situation; don't let it come to throwing elbows, silent threats, or passive-aggressive commentary.

DON'T GET WASTED ON THE PLANE OR IN THE AIRPORT
Don't be that person that knocks themselves out with liquor; it's not only frowned upon but they might not let you on your flight. We've all seen videos of people puking in the lounge area or passed out before boarding and it's just not a great look (and you'll feel like crap at your destination). Take prescribed medication if flying is an issue for you and don't be a drunk nuisance to staff and other passengers. They didn't ask to deal with you.

On another note—hell yeah you can drink in the airport or on a plane. Airports are a sacred place where crack of dawn breakfast wine isn't frowned upon.

If you're looking to bring booze on the plane, per current TSA regulations you're allowed to bring as many airplane bottles (1.7 ounce bottles but you can go up to 3.4 ounces) that will comfortably fit in a quart sized, clear plastic, zip-top bag. You can also bring on bottles you bought after clearing security, which is pretty clutch if you're traveling internationally and scored a duty-free bottle.

The catch is that you're technically only allowed to bring bottles in your carry-on, but not drink them. Per FAA regulations, "No person may drink any alcoholic beverage aboard an aircraft unless the certificate holder operating the aircraft has served that beverage." If you break that rule, you can snag up to an $11,000 fine.

This leaves you with some options: drink the booze you brought on the sly and hide the bottles, or purchase booze from your flight attendants. So you're not hit with a massive fine and blame me for it, I advocate buying the booze.

Here are just a few mixed drinks you can make with complimentary drinks from the airline.

◆ **White Russian**
Baileys Irish Cream
Vodka
Complimentary half and half

◆ **Screwdriver**
Vodka
Complimentary orange juice

◆ **Cape Codder**
Vodka
Complimentary Cranberry juice

There are a ton of other variations, ranging from the ubiquitous vodka soda or gin and tonic to more elaborate creations you can make with those flight cocktail kits, but I'm personally more of a minimalist when I'm several thousand feet in the air.

CHAPTER 3

Career

Interviewer: "What's one of your strongest skills?"

"My ability to hit it and quit it."

Interviewer: "We were hoping for someone who was proficient in Excel."

Your career is just that: yours. To a certain degree, you can do whatever the hell you want with it, which is both liberating and terrifying all at once. The important thing is to take it day by day and remember that a job is a paycheck and not the be-all and end-all of your life.

There's always a fear of not living up to your own potential, and we all have it. The good and bad news is that your potential is unlimited so you can be both pleased and disappointed with yourself all at once, which is healthy and normal. Even the most successful people you know are probably kicking themselves over a deal gone wrong or something they could have done better, regardless of how much you think they exemplify the ultimate in their chosen field.

Another important thing to remember is that *your career is only one facet of your life*. That's why people stress a work/life balance so much—people that only focus on their career don't really have a life. If you're reading this book, you're likely starting out in your career and have already figured out what you want to do and are moving towards set goals and milestones. Or you're just going through the motions until you figure out exactly what it is you really want to do. While the former is preferable for your own peace of mind, who are we kidding, the latter is all of us. Even the people who think they have it all figured out might make a career pivot after realizing what they actually want to pursue.

We're all on separate schedules and paces; don't let Facebook updates about promotions and the *Forbes* "30 Under 30" list make you feel like shit. Most awards for professionals are little more than a circle jerk anyway. With that visual in mind, let's move forward.

DECIDING WHAT YOU WANT TO DO

This is a little more involved than throwing a dart at a board and going from there.

You have to figure out:

WHAT YOU'RE GOOD AT

This is where left brain/right brain characteristics come in. If you're good at math and science, you should consider a more data-driven job, like finance, engineering, or a medical profession. If you're good at writing and reading, then consider something in marketing, communications, or any of the entertainment industry jobs that will make your family regret funding a private school education.

WHAT ISN'T GOING TO MAKE YOU WANT TO JUMP OUT A WINDOW

Jobs are repetitive by nature because...it's a job. You wake up every day and go to work, oftentimes completing the same task over and over again, like a hamster on a wheel but with forced office happy hours. That "love what you'll do and you'll never work a day in your life" line is complete bullshit—everyone hates what they do sometimes. The trick is finding something you can enjoy sometimes or at least tolerate enough that you don't have a complete mental breakdown by 26. (Which you're totally still allowed to do even if you like your job—mine involved sitting by my friend's pool in LA for a week while double fisting baguettes and vodka. I regret nothing.)

HOW MUCH MONEY YOU WANT TO MAKE

A lot of people will tell you that your salary doesn't matter and as a writer I'm here to tell you *it does*.

Want to lead a comfortable lifestyle? Go for a job that will at least pay decently and isn't notorious for laying people off in droves, or might be gone in a few years as artificial intelligence improves.

As someone who really likes what they do for a living now, I'm still not sure I would tell my younger self to pursue the jobs I did. I've gone through a lot of phases when I've had freelance jobs on top of full-time employment, and shitty living situations you couldn't pay me enough to relive. There's something to be said about pursuing your dream career on your own time if it's not financially realistic—at least until you feel like you can make it your full-time gig.

We're all just a few breakdowns away from becoming an interior designer or a golf pro.

"How do you like my résumé?"

"You just handed me a bunch of vague threats scribbled on a cocktail napkin."

"Exactly."

If you want to pursue a career that is notorious for low pay but actually does some impact in this world, like at a non-profit or as a social worker, then honestly good for you and I salute you for trying to make the world a better place; we need all the help we can get.

RÉSUMÉ

The first step to getting a job is landing an interview. And to land an interview, regardless of how much job experience you have, you're going to need some basic things at the ready—like your résumé and cover letter.

I'm not going to bore you with a sample résumé because there are a million templates online, but bear in mind it's usually not a human being that's reading your résumé. Unless you're being referred by a friend, colleague, or friend/colleague of your parent (abuse those relationships whenever you possibly can, nepotism always wins), your résumé is being dumped into a program that's scanning it for keywords that match the job description.

This is why it's not a bad idea to have multiple résumés, each tailored to specific roles you want. A rule of thumb is to look at the job description of your dreams, and include as many of those same keywords and skills listed in your résumé, as long as it's true. It's important to have a nice looking résumé that's cohesive and easily readable with mature fonts, but don't stress if it's not something that deserves to be hung in the Met. The AI program or hiring manager won't give a crap.

Another word of warning is to always save both word docs and PDFs of your résumés. When you want to quickly update your résumé to send out, you don't want to have to redo the whole thing—keep the original or a copy so you don't hate yourself every few months or years.

Will Sparks, a technical recruiter at Google notes, "It helps to have a blue-chip company on your résumé because the best companies often hire the best people, given the competition to work for them. They also tend to have proven recruiting processes that weed out the weak candidates."

If you can financially take a hit, getting the good company on your résumé over a higher paying yet unknown startup might be a better bet for your career path when you're first starting out. From personal experience, I know the legacy brands on my résumé are the ones that usually get my foot in the next door.

Other tips: 🖊

- Keep your résumé to a page or less unless you have at least seven years of experience, but even then, tailor it to be shorter. No one wants to read a novel about your Excel skills and email open rates.

- Leave off any summer jobs or irrelevant things you've done to make it look longer. No one cares about those few months you spent getting high with the other waiters.

- Take off your graduation date if you're worried about age discrimination.

- Make a vanity (more official looking) email address that doesn't include Gmail, Yahoo, or (God forbid) AOL URL. This is free, easy, and you can funnel your Gmail account through it. You can also personalize your LinkedIn with a vanity URL as well. This makes you look exceedingly more professional with minimal effort, which is ideal, tbh.

- Please don't list your hobbies and interests. This should be a given, but when you're looking to fill up space, who knows what dark path you'll be led down.

- Focus on highlighting your achievements during the time in your job or internship, rather than your responsibilities. Be able to quantify them or at least illustrate why you were invaluable. For example, instead of saying that you managed the intern program, talk about the activities you led and how many interns you managed.

COVER LETTER 🖇

Ah yes, the unique-to-you cover letter. You should always include one if it's asked for, and once you have a template saved it's easy to replace the company name and job title along with rearranging key roles and skills that match the job description. That said, if you're obsessed

> **The ten happiest professions are also some of the lesser paid ones. Clearly these people have not felt the joy of cashmere.**

with the company and really, really want the job—go ahead and personalize it to your heart's content.

A rule of thumb is to include attributes, skills, or cool, professionally-skewed, unique things about yourself. Leave off your beer pong league, but things like volunteering or a side hustle will inject personality into an otherwise notoriously bland document. You are so much more than your past job experience, and here's your chance to tell HR or the hiring manager how and why.

Add your contact information at the top so they can get in touch with you easily, and double, triple check to make sure that it is right. While a cover letter should always be professional, it shouldn't sound like a form letter. If you're not addressing a specific person, then just skip the greeting altogether to avoid the dreaded "To Whom it May Concern."

In the brief opening paragraph, speak about the position and succinctly say why you're a great fit.

In the main part of the paragraph, sell yourself to the company and to the specific role, giving concrete examples of your achievements and how they would carry themselves well into this job. Don't give them your whole life story, but get the point across (without sounding overconfident). You may be tempted to write out an extended version of your résumé, but try not to be repetitive.

In the closing paragraph, concisely reiterate why you'd be interested in the position, and formally sign off with "sincerely" or "respectfully." I always tend to include my website and portfolio links, but this isn't applicable for all professions.

INTERVIEWS

Interviews are a lot like a first date. You're slightly anxious, not sure if you really want to be there, and the other person isn't positive about you either. Like dates, you should always put your best foot forward sartorially, not reveal too much, and don't bash your exes (which in this case are past jobs).

There are usually going to be several rounds of interviews based on the company's hiring protocol and how elevated the position will be.

At the most, you'll have to get through a HR

Email from HR: "Can you please remove the sign on your cubicle that says 'welcome to the glass ceiling.'"

phone screening, another phone screening with the hiring manager, an in-house interview with one or several people, test(s) relevant to the task or job you're interviewing for, and then some more in-house interviews with even more elevated executives, such as a VP or the CEO or owner of the company. Hiring someone is a big, expensive deal and the HR team is going to make you jump through multiple hoops to see if you're the right fit for the company.

If reading that paragraph made you tired, then think of performing the same tasks over and over again if you're interviewing at multiple places. The good news is that it's a repetitive process, and you'll become a pro or at least proficient in interviewing sooner than you think.

Step 1: *Don't screw up the phone screening*

Unless you're directly speaking to the hiring manager, the phone screening by a HR person or qualified member of the team is just to see if you have the right job experience, can perform under pressure, and are competent and sane. You can and will rock this.

Step 2: *Write "thank you" notes after every interview*

Even if it was only a phone interview! Send a follow-up email within 24 hours of your speaking or meeting with the person in question, thanking them for their time.

Here's a sample "thank you" that you're welcome to steal. Just remember to tailor it to each individual you interviewed with, and refer to something you spoke about in the interview that will jog their memory and help make you stand out.

> Dear *blank*,
>
> Thanks for taking the time to chat yesterday, it was great to hear more about *company* and *something that relates back to the interview*. If you'd like more examples of my past work please don't hesitate to ask, and I'm looking forward to connecting again!
>
> Sincerely,
> *You, the person who will get this job.*

QUESTIONS TO ASK DURING THE INTERVIEW

Without fail, an interviewer will ask if you have any questions for them. And with good reason! You'll potentially be spending the majority of your time working for this company, and should do your due diligence about work hours, company culture, expectations for answering late-night and weekend emails, and dress code. While the latter seems shallow, revamping your entire office wardrobe for a job you're not thrilled about could be reason enough for you to keep looking.

It's not a good look to be caught off-guard with questions at the end—I know I have—so here are some sure fire ones that will make you seem like the competent professional you are.

- **What are some qualities an ideal candidate for this position would possess?**
  This way, you can bring up how you mirror some of those qualities.

- **What are some of the largest challenges I would face in this position?**
  This is for your own knowledge, and you can offer some past experiences in which you've triumphed over similar instances.

- **How would you measure success for this position?**
  Also extremely helpful, because this is when they'll tell you what they're actually looking for without a lot of the unnecessary jargon included in the job description.

- **Is there upward mobility with this role?**
  At our age, sometimes there isn't. I've been at jobs where they point-blank told me this was the end of the road in my department. And you need to figure out if that's okay for you—if you want to work for a company that you can grow with, or a company that's okay for right now.

- **What's the timeline for next steps?**
  This is extremely important for your own peace of mind. Some places will hire you the next week and others can take months to even get the ball rolling. By having an idea of when they'll contact you next, you can rest easier and also follow up after that tentative deadline has passed. It's not rude to email HR or the hiring manager a few weeks later with a, "Just circling back because I wanted to reiterate my interest in this position" message.

SALARY NEGOTIATION

Ah yes, the lovely discussion of your worth. It may seem harrowing at first and you may feel uncomfortable or loathe to speak up, but this is a big fucking deal. Even just a small bump in salary could mean a better apartment, nicer car, or peace of mind from having money in the bank.

It's always best to have three numbers in mind: what you really want, what you'll take, and what you'll walk away from. Remember that it's always easier to negotiate down than up.

To get those numbers, you should do your research—both online and with colleagues in a similar company or field. When they ask how you came to this number, tell them you've not only done your due diligence online but with colleagues.

If you've recently graduated or don't have a ton of experience, it may be harder to negotiate, *but you should always try*. There's the cost of living to consider, plus whatever student loans you're carrying on your (very tired) back.

Alicia McElhaney, founder at She Spends and finance journalist, helped highlight why you *need* to negotiate, even if it's your first job. "When I first started working as a reporter, I struggled to make rent in New York. I took on side hustles like walking dogs and selling my clothes on Poshmark, and it was hard. I wish I had asked my first boss for more money when I started out, but I didn't know how to do it, and I was intimidated by the boys club that financial reporting turned out to be. The best financial advice I can give to someone starting out is to negotiate your salary, no matter what type of job you're taking on. The worst thing a potential employer can do is say no."

Pro tip: When you're applying for jobs, don't put your desired salary when they ask how much you'd want. Put "0" or, "I'm happy to discuss once we clarify the responsibilities of the job," so they don't toss out your application if your number wasn't in their range. Sometimes that number can shift if they really like you.

JOB REJECTIONS ✖

When you're applying to a bunch of jobs online it's normal and expected to receive a flurry of rejection emails in the coming days, weeks, and months. This does not reflect who you are as a person! You are a delightful creature who deserves to be employed by the best of the best. More often than not, the algorithm blindly didn't think you were a good fit, a current employee was promoted internally, or someone knew a friend of a friend and jumped the interview line. Which leads me to...

YOUR CONNECTIONS ARE YOUR BEST ASSETS

I can't even tell you the number of times my application was overlooked by HR and then I suddenly got a phone call or email because

Probably should take "send n00dz" out of my professional email signature.

Considering Manhattan is an island, this is the least relaxing extended vacation ever.

Proud to have made 30 Under-achievers Under 30 Barely Skirting by Thanks to a Decent Vocabulary and Rack.

a friend gave an internal reference. You actually knowing someone at the company increases your chances of getting your foot in the door by at least 300%. (I made that percentage up, but what percentage isn't fabricated?)

It's an unfair practice but unfortunately, that's the way life works. Most of my jobs, both full-time and contract, have been through connections, and a lot of my friends can say the same. I've also gotten jobs through Twitter by posting that I was suddenly and unexpectedly unemployed, and through looking up whom I knew at specific companies through the magic of LinkedIn. More often than not, people will want to help you out, either because they're a decent person or because they expect you to return the favor someday. There's also a beautiful thing known as the referral bonus, where if you get hired full-time the friend who referred you will get a chunk of change in their next paycheck, so that's extra impetus for them to recruit you.

If your friend happens to score you a job, buy 'em a drink or dinner. Or let them buy you one if their referral bonus was insane.

SOCIAL MEDIA

WHEN YOU SHOULD LOCK YOUR ACCOUNTS

Ah yes, the decision to lock any of your social media accounts is a double-edged sword. On the one hand, you may not gain the following you want on platforms like Twitter where the more your content is shared the larger a following you'll acquire, whereas on Instagram some of the more popular accounts are locked because they want to force you to follow them. (This is to prevent you aimlessly scrolling through their page when you want a laugh or to check out their #content.)

Aspiring meme lords and creative types *should not* be on lockdown. I can't tell you the number of times I've been asked for my social handles while applying for a job, or one of the conditions of the job is to be an "influencer" on at least one platform.* It's both sad and unfair, but that's the world we're subjected to now. All the world's a stage and employers want to abuse the hell out of your social networks with their content.

* However, I do mainly apply to content- and social media-related jobs.

"If you don't promote yourself, who will?" she said, handing a temporary tattoo of her food blog Instagram handle to a homeless person.

If you're working in finance, the sciences, or anything that doesn't require you to be an advocate in your field (or your social handles aren't part of your overall work portfolio), then locking them might be a good idea—especially if you tend to get drunk and post stupid things. If you don't particularly care about anyone besides your actual friends seeing what you're posting, you're avoiding any headaches or compliance issues with your employer by locking your accounts. I know I've *definitely* been passed over for jobs (and dates) because of my social media presence. I'm a blazing red flag in many respects, but that's part of my charm, I guess.

Suppose you're in a "left brain" field and want to be an advocate for your profession, or have a social presence when potential clients Google you, because it makes you look more human and trustworthy. If you're someone public-facing like a doctor or financial advisor who can restrain themselves from posting less than professional content, it's perfectly advisable and even preferable to stay unlocked. Plus, social media is fun and a great way to interact with people with similar interests.

DON'T TWEET, 'GRAM, OR POST ANYTHING AFTER TWO DRINKS

This is the rule of thumb when I post for brands, but it should also go for your own accounts because, unfortunately, you are your own personal brand. In our current state of affairs (people getting riled up over literally anything and everything posted online), even if you delete something the next morning it was probably screen-grabbed.

Save yourself the heartache and possible HR trip by abstaining from posting controversial content on your unlocked account if you have something to lose.

HARNESSING LINKEDIN

Ah yes, the most obnoxious of social platforms is also the most useful while job-hunting. As tedious as it is, creating a respectable page, and adding the people you know, and asking your supervisors to post references to your page is highly advised.

The key to using LinkedIn is looking up dream companies or brands you'd

Apparently you get reported to LinkedIn for endorsing people as your "eskimo brothers."

like to work for and seeing if they have any employees that you're already connected to, or who are a friend of a friend to help you get your foot in the door. *A referral from an employee is what makes all the difference between a human never seeing your application and it getting into the hands of the appropriate people.*

If this is sincerely your dream job and you feel like it would be a good fit, but you don't have any connections at the company, find the recruiter on LinkedIn and send a cold InMail.

An example of a message to a recruiter or HR professional:

Hi *blank*,

Hope you're having a good week! (Or insert other generic pleasantry.) I apologize for the cold InMail but I wanted to reach out concerning the *blank* role because I feel that I would be an excellent fit.

She felt a soft chill and shuddered. The finance interns had gone back to school.

Then go into your past experience and skills, but keep it short; the whole message shouldn't be longer than three paragraphs max. Remember, they can easily just look at your LinkedIn page.

An obvious side note, but needed nonetheless: LinkedIn is like Facebook for job-seekers and consummate professionals, so keep your page strictly work related. And for the love of God, use it as a professional tool, not a dating site. It's not uncommon to get messages from people trying to use it as yet another dating app and, while I admire their ingenuity and persistence, don't be that thirsty.

HOW TO TURN THAT INTERNSHIP INTO A JOB

To put it simply: do a good job and stay in touch. It's that easy. I personally love it when my former interns pop up out of the woodwork to say hello. If you spent a decent amount of time with employees over the course of your internship, the odds are they looked at you as a coworker rather than an intern, and will go to bat with HR for you.

If you decide you don't like the place you interned for, then consider that one more company you've crossed off your list. Good or bad, it was still experience, and you can reach out to your former supervisors regarding career advice, references, and to ask them to help you with specific companies where they have connections.

Probably shouldn't have told that guy in the kitchen reading *Atlas Shrugged* to, "Do less."

TAKE CONSTRUCTIVE CRITICISM SERIOUSLY

We all dread it—knowing you screwed up in some capacity and are going to be pulled into a room by your boss and given a stern talking to. We've all been there, whether you accidentally sent an inappropriate joke from the corporate social media account or you actually need to take your daily morning meeting seriously and not like your personal time to mainline coffee. *cough* Been there, done that. *cough*

Unfortunately (or fortunately), this is a learning experience and should be taken as such. Bear in mind, your boss probably sucks at giving negative feedback because they're going to get in trouble for your actions and are taking it out on you, and/or they feel guilty talking down to you because they genuinely like you and your work.

As difficult as it may be, take the criticism seriously and frame it as a way to improve your work. Later on, you can mark it down on your achievements sheet that we mention later in the chapter—like, "You told me I did X,Y, and Z incorrectly and I really took it to heart and improved my work performance."

Remember to always play the system, don't let the system play you. *nonchalantly flips hair*

SHORT-TERM VERSUS LONG-TERM GOALS/HOW TO ANSWER THE 5-YEAR PLAN QUESTION

In a nutshell, your short-term goals feed into your long-term goals, ultimately leading to what you *really* want to do.

Probably shouldn't dress as my "5-year plan" for the office Halloween party tomorrow and show up in resort wear.

For example, "I want to have 'fuck you' money and retire at 45" is a long-term goal. A short-term goal would be: nailing an interview that would lead to the job you want.

This leads to the age-old question, "Where do you see yourself in five years?" If a hiring manager has the audacity to ask you about such a fluid concept, it may be tempting to go with an old standby (quickly replying that you'd like to be in their position) or the truth ("Have you been paying attention to the news? We may not have five years!").

Don't do either. There are a few ways to nimbly answer this:

- If you're really not sure, say your experience in this position would help solidify your future because you're interested in X,Y,Z and definitely see yourself in this career path.

- Be realistically specific to the position and align yourself with a role in that company that makes sense, five years down the road.

- If you don't know enough about the company's hierarchy, just say something along the lines of, "With the experience I would garner in this position, I would hope to be in a more managerial role at this company."

Remember to tie everything back to how this position leads to your long-term goals, hiring managers aren't thrilled with people that reek of Peter Pan syndrome.

Meanwhile, on your own time, write down and work at hitting your (real) short-term goals. Only focusing on your long-term ones isn't feasible, and will drive you insane. Rome wasn't built in a day, it took hundreds of years of slave labor.

MENTAL HEALTH DAYS—THEY'RE LEGIT!

Everyone gets burned out, regardless of your field or profession, and the only way to combat that drained, empty, and sullen feeling is to take some damn time off.

There's nothing wrong with you; it's a universal feeling. The important thing is to not do anything drastic while you're feeling burned out, like have an existential crisis and quit your job to audition to be a SoulCycle instructor when you've only taken two classes.

After some time in the workforce, you'll learn when you need to schedule mental health days ahead of time so you don't question your own sanity every few months. Mental health days should usually be reserved for something that makes you genuinely happy and well-rested, like getting a massage, eating at your favorite restaurant in the middle of the day without worrying about a reservation, or refusing to leave your bed. It's all up to you because it's *your* day and no one can take those few sacred hours away from you.

Conversely, schedule a vacation to truly escape it all. Even getting on a train for a day trip makes a world of difference.

When I'm feeling particularly overwhelmed and sick of work, I'll walk through the park and sit in the grass with a book and refuse to answer texts, no matter how hot the guy sending them is. Bodies of water are also particularly cathartic when you need something to mindlessly stare it; just remember to fight the urge to throw any and all electronic devices in them.

BE GRATEFUL FOR YOUR JOB

This is something to remember during your darkest hours under the company roof or co-working space: even after all the bullshit your job has put you through, it's still (hopefully) paying the bills. Unemployment sucks and job-hunting sucks; never forget those two little nuggets of information when you're daydreaming about stealing all the office supplies for personal Pinterest projects, flipping off your boss, walking out of the building, and never coming back.

"Self-care is my favorite sport because I always come in first," she announced.

Cashier: "Miss, did you want the large fries with your nuggets or not?"

Is the new American dream to work remotely?

If you're feeling particularly ungrateful, that's a huge burnout red flag and it's crucial to schedule a vacation or some time off. If it persists, then it may be time to start looking for a new job that's better suited to your tastes, interests, and goals. And no, becoming the "corgi rescue center" of New England because you're getting tired of your analyst position isn't a good idea.

My only new year's resolution is to stop blurting out "That's what she said" in professional settings.

OPEN OFFICE FLOOR PLANS

More often than not, you're going to be faced with an open office floor plan. It's mainly a cubicle-less space, usually where you're seated on long tables next to your coworkers. Like everything you're faced with on a daily basis, there are both pros and cons to this environment.

Pros	Cons
• More interaction with coworkers	• Everyone can see your computer
• More "face time" with superiors	• Little to no privacy
• Usually more aesthetically pleasing	• More "face time" with superiors
• More collaborative	• You can't decorate as much as you could with a cubicle
• When an office happy hour starts, everyone is kind of forced to stop	• Everyone can see when you arrive and leave
	• When an office happy hour starts, everyone is kind of forced to stop

Personally, I feel that open office floor plans are the devil, but I've learned to live with them out of necessity. If you're feeling particularly overwhelmed in a certain area or a coworker is being unnecessarily loud, usually there are open rooms for you to run into to finish an assignment or take a call. If the problem becomes persistent, that's when you need to speak to your manager or team members about a better seating solution in another section of the office. More often than not, they'll share the same grievances and the issue can be solved.

"Why did you get a bad work performance review?"

"I forgot it was that day and wore my 'Sorry I'm late— I don't want to be here' tee."

REVIEW TIME

This is where showing up on time and not noticeably hungover comes into play.

The annual review is when you have to prove your worth to the company (and, more specifically, your manager), and when they tell you the areas in which you can improve. It's important to be humble in your review, but also state how and why you're an asset to the company, so you can potentially unlock your bonus and a performance-based raise.

There are a few ways this can go:

- They tell you you're doing an excellent job and to keep up the good work.
- You'll discuss where you're performing well and what you can improve upon (this is most likely).
- They'll tell you you're in serious danger of being let go.

If you're in the third camp—don't ask for a raise. If you're in one of the first two, it's not obnoxious to ask for a raise once a year. Otherwise it's not unusual to get a ~2% bump without asking, just for making it through the year.

If you ask and don't receive a raise, or they're being tight for any number of reasons, you can ask for things that aren't tied to a monetary amount but will increase your quality of life, like: more time off, the ability to work remotely a certain number of days a week or month, or conferences you want to attend.

Pro tip: So you're not scrambling right before your review to number the reasons why you're the best and the brightest there is—always keep a document handy to jot down any notable achievements and successes. This is so you're armed and ready for any questions about your worth.

If you're a freelance or contract worker, I suggest *always* keeping a list of

If someone listed their job on a dating app as "entrepreneur," just assume they're unemployed.

what you worked on that day in case they dispute your invoice. When I email an invoice I'll also include a running list of what I worked on in the body copy during those hours, so they won't call bullshit. Companies *love* to argue with contract workers about their hours.

:(WE ARE ALL EXPENDABLE CREW MEMBERS

If you've ever watched an iconic show like *Star Trek*, you're aware that unnamed, otherwise unimportant crew members are always offed first during any attack or battle sequence. Those are colloquially referred to as the "expendable crew members," and if you're working for a larger corporation—congrats! You are one as well.

You may love your company and the feeling may be mutual, but know when things go poorly, no one is safe. Unless you know someone extremely high up, as far as the consultant or accountant doing the dirty work of figuring out whom to cut is concerned, your ass is grass. The important thing to remember is to never take being let go for financial reasons too personally, and to take any lovey-dovey corporate culture stuff with a grain of salt. Your company may offer you catered lunches and free beer but, as soon as things take a turn for the worse, it's every man or woman for themselves.

Why did HR call you in?"

"They asked me stop blatantly turning the empty cubicle next to me into a Bloody Mary bar."

DON'T TIE YOUR SELF-WORTH TO YOUR JOB

This is one of the hardest and most important feats to accomplish, because we all too often define ourselves by what we do for a living. It's one of the first things people ask when they meet you, it's where and how you spend most of your waking hours, and it's the magical, albeit exhausting, thing that funds the other facets of your life.

Some of the most successful people I know worked shitty, tiresome, and unglamorous gigs before they caught a break. Other people I know work day jobs that aren't exactly their passion, because the work they do on their own time is what they're gung ho about. You have to do what's right for your financial situation until you can get to a point where doing what you love is also what pays the bills. Until then, do whatever is necessary to keep a roof over your head and the lights on.

A former coworker and recent Penn State graduate, Dan Kuhn, states the one thing he wished he had known before starting his first full-time job very eloquently and succinctly. "It's an ongoing lesson, but I wish I hadn't tied so much of my self-worth to an idealized version of a job. Good job or bad job, love yourself for the terrible person you are."

You are so much more than your job; try never to forget that.

"How's unemployment going?" "Thanks to all the additional face mask time, my skin has never looked better."

GETTING LAID OFF

Ah yes, the lovely walk to HR and being handed a bunch of paperwork to "look over" while tech is locking your computer so you don't revenge-steal confidential files. Been there! It's a turbulent time for so many legacy fields and, as the economy fluctuates, employees are let go in droves. It's not fair or kind, but you learn to deal with it the only way you can—you move the fuck on.

The important thing is not to lose your shit, because you never know whom you're going to need to ask for a reference or whom can reach out and help get your foot in the door somewhere else. Coolly take the paperwork, pack your shit up, say goodbye to the people you were close with (or just see them later), and get the hell out of there. On the bright side, you get to go home.

Crack a beer, light a joint, and do whatever you have to calm down. To steal a line from the Disney classic *Aladdin*, "Genie, you're free."

OUTSIDE THE GOLDMAN SACHS PROTEST

"Why did you write your phone number on a poster?"

UNEMPLOYMENT CHECKLIST

In the words of my mother, one of the most badass women I know: "Work now, freak later." Now that you don't have an income, you have to spring into action to find something that will both complement your skill set and compensate you fairly, if not well. Your degenerate lifestyle doesn't fund itself!

Some general steps you should take the same week if not immediately after being let go:

ALERT YOUR NETWORK THAT YOU'RE LOOKING FOR WORK

Your first line of offense is your network. They'll help get the ball rolling for you by letting you know of open roles at their company, or at least pass your info along in case someone mentions they're looking for a quality candidate. If you have a social following and don't have qualms about posting that you were let go, this is often the quickest and easiest course of action.

IF YOU GOT A SEVERANCE PACKAGE, REALLY LOOK IT OVER BEFORE SIGNING

In exchange for you unceremoniously being let go from your full-time position, you'll often get a few weeks' or months' pay in one lump sum (taxed) in exchange for your signing a non-disclosure agreement (NDA).

An NDA will make sure you don't disclose confidential information or knowledge about the company. Usually there's something in there stating that you can't publicly speak ill of the company for a certain amount of time (or like, ever). In short, they're buying your silence.

I've had coworkers dispute their severance and get larger sums of money, but they were higher up than me and had worked at places for far longer. If you don't feel like playing nice and think the amount of money they offered

World's smallest violin

you as severance is an insult, then don't sign it and really go to town on them with lawyers. They fucked with your livelihood, feel free to return the favor.

You can usually get pro bono lawyers through the state, but you have to qualify as low-income. Unfortunately, as lawyers are extremely expensive, it's likely in your best interests to sign the NDA and move on with your life. Yayyy for late-stage capitalism.

APPLY FOR UNEMPLOYMENT
We all pay into the system, now it's time to see if you can get a helping hand from it. If you received severance you're often not qualified for unemployment until it runs out or until the month after it runs out. There's a lot of tricky timing involved so apply as soon as you possibly can.

APPLY FOR ASSISTED HEALTH INSURANCE
Health insurance is one of those obnoxious but incredibly necessary costs. If something happens to you, God forbid, a hospital bill sans-insurance could cripple you financially for the rest of your life. Go to the Medicaid and other assisted health insurance online marketplaces and see what you're qualified for—if you're totally screwed, at least you can get health insurance at a lower cost.

MAKE A NEW BUDGET
With a drastic change in income comes a new mentality about spending. Yay! Make a checklist of everything you *need* to spend money on such as rent,

utilities, groceries, your credit card bills, insurance, and any debt, along with how much "fun" cash you'll allow yourself so you don't go completely insane.

It's also time to rethink the things in your life that are great when you have the cash flow, but is a $300-a-month gym membership worth it for the stellar steam rooms and eucalyptus-scented towels? Everyone has their own deeply personal financial situation, and it's up to you to decide what you're cutting back on. There will most likely be fewer dinners out and less extravagant vacations, but don't become an absolute martyr. You've got to keep a balance between conscious spending and still enjoying yourself. Who knows when you'll next have this much time off work?

DON'T BE TOO HARD ON YOURSELF

Getting laid off happens to the best of us. Stay positive, focus on the task at hand, and just keep swimming. Some days it may feel like a positively insurmountable task to even get out of bed, but you will get through this—with sheer perseverance, and by channeling all that anger and fear into your application and interview game.

> It was so warm out today I got to have my existential crisis outside.

KEEP A SCHEDULE

By waking up and going to bed at a similar time as you did when you had a job, you can maintain some semblance of a schedule, so that you're not completely miserable when you do start working again. It also helps to stay sober during work hours, so you don't downward-spiral or end up bingeing all of *Arrested Development* for the fourth time. By all means, enjoy your newfound freedom, but within reason, and don't make getting wasted at al fresco lunches a near-daily habit. That's what retirement is for.

DO WHATEVER YOU HAVE TO DO

Only you know what gigs you're willing to take if you need money. Life is hard enough, don't let other people's judgment get in the way of your making rent and keeping two varieties of cheese in your fridge at all times.

Pro tip: If you want to take some time off before you begin your job search, that's between you and your savings account, but it does get harder to snag interviews and ultimately land jobs the longer you wait. No one said being an adult was fun or easy, and this fact is definitely a testament to that.

THINK HARD ABOUT JUMPING FROM JOB TO JOB

Sometimes the only way to get a raise is to leave for another company. Don't be complacent and shrug your shoulders if your cost of living suddenly goes up—do something about it. Always remember: No one is going to fix your circumstances but you.

According to a 2018 Deloitte survey of 10,455 millennials, 43% were planning on leaving their job within two years, as opposed to 38% the year before. That's nearly half of the demographic planning to jump ship, on an upward trending trajectory.

The downside to hopping around is that you become less appealing to recruiters and to companies that want to see you in a role for longer than a year or two. Will Sparks, a technical recruiter at Google, shared his thoughts on finding stellar candidates:

> "First and foremost you want someone who has distinguished themselves. Meaning—have they done something in their career or at university that was significant and made them stand out from their peers or coworkers? Ideally, you want someone who has showed some loyalty and hasn't jumped around in their career, but more importantly, you want someone who has demonstrated a forward career trajectory and progress at their respective companies. You want people who have drive and are willing to work hard, or are passionate enough about something that they are willing to go above and beyond their normal job duties."

The people that post inspirational quotes online don't have to deal with the subway.

Don't leave your job for a silly reason—it has to be for your career development, work/life balance, or a big bump in pay.

DON'T BE OBVIOUS THAT YOU'RE INTERVIEWING

While you may emotionally be on your way out, and think the next job is lined up, for the love of God do not say anything until you have the new employment contract signed, sealed, and delivered. Your current job is still your source of income, and that is something to respect and defer to until you're at your next gig.

I can't tell you the number of times I thought an interview had gone superbly and they would be clamoring to hire me, only to be told they went in a different direction or promoted someone internally. Never assume anything; there are too many variables and you're not present for the discussions going on behind closed doors.

So, how should you build out an interviewing game plan while still putting 100% into your full-time job?

- **Be as discreet as possible**—don't dress up differently on the days you have a "dentist appointment." Bring your interview clothes in a gym bag along with a travel garment steamer if you need to, or schedule interviews in the morning or the late afternoon so you can change and keep a somewhat normal work schedule, which brings us to...

- **Don't try to schedule interviews during lunch** (unless they're within walking distance). Interviews will often run over and you don't want to rush through them in a vain attempt to get back to an afternoon meeting. That screws up your interview, and you'll probably be late for your meeting anyway.

- **Have a plan of action if your boss asks if you're looking around.** Don't have the "I'm planning on quitting" conversation before you're ready—it's awkward and your boss won't trust you afterwards. Besides, what if you end up not taking the job? There are so many last-minute contract negotiations to consider that may change your mind.

- **Turn off your LinkedIn notifications to your network.** Everyone in your network will be able to see you're connecting with recruiters, adding connections from a specific company, or just being more active than usual. At the very least, they'll wonder whether something's up.

Probably should change my out-of-office reply from "I don't have the emotional bandwidth for this."

EMAIL BEST PRACTICES

The nuances of business emails mean a lot more than you would think. Oftentimes, you'll mainly communicate with coworkers through email if they're working out of another office, and their impression of you will be a combination of how you word emails and your response time.

To help you navigate those murky waters, here are some email best practices—because your boss probably won't appreciate you mainly corresponding through Kardashian GIFs.

STATE THE INTENT OF THE EMAIL IN THE SUBJECT LINE

This makes it easier for both the person receiving it, so they can prioritize it better, and you, so it's easier to search and find later. Take care—writing the subject line in all caps, all lowercase, or with excessive punctuation makes it a spam red flag.

DON'T EMAIL ANGRY

You'll regret it in about 20 minutes when you've cooled off. Sometimes I'll write the angry email version to amuse myself and get it out of my system, then I'll delete all of the vague threats and attacks against their personal style and rewrite it in a much more calm and contained manner.

DON'T HIT "REPLY ALL" UNLESS YOU NEED TO

Everyone will hate you for all the unnecessary commentary in their inbox—only "reply all" if everyone else is doing it, the team would appreciate it, or they need to see your paper trail.

BCC IS YOUR FRIEND

If you don't want to share the email addresses of everyone you're sending the message to, then bcc the names you want hidden.

If you've been introduced to someone over email and it's not necessary to include your friend in future correspondence, thank them and say that you're moving them to bcc. You're acknowledging that you've received the introduction and plan on speaking to the other person, but now they don't have to see all the emails. Your friend or colleague did you a favor; don't unnecessarily clog their inbox.

DON'T USE TOO MANY EXCLAMATION POINTS

You'll look scarily enthusiastic. Please don't.

DON'T USE EMOJIS

There's a time or a place for emojis, and it's not in a professional setting.

KEEP IT SHORT

No one likes to read a novel in their inbox. If an email looks intimidatingly long, the recipient might save it for later (and promptly forget about it) because they don't feel like tackling something that verbose at the moment.

HAVE A PROFESSIONAL-LOOKING SIGNATURE

If it's your business email, then include the company standard signature and add your personal details. If it's your own, add your

In Hell, they only let you eat lunches you meal-prepped.

website and phone number; there should be another way to contact you outside of the provided email address.

THE WORDING SHOULD REFLECT WHOM YOU'RE SENDING THE EMAIL TO
Are they super important in your company, or are they your intern who just refused to get you coffee? You can be less thoughtful in the editing process when it comes to the ungrateful intern.

If the person you're sending it to is formal, write in that tone. If they're pretty informal, they'll respect a more colloquial email. Just remember to not write anything even remotely inappropriate while using company email; the business is allowed to look at anything and everything and you don't want it to come back to bite you in the ass.

Just had to compete in an office Easter egg hunt, as if I'm not constantly reminded of my fleeting childbearing years already.

MEAL-PREP BASICS

You don't need me to lecture you on why you should bring your lunch instead of buying it every day. You'll save around $50 a week ($200 a month), which isn't a small chunk of change. It's also considerably healthier, because you control what's going in your lunch instead of turning to better tasting, more caloric food in times of stress. Plus, your considerate coworkers are always going to pressure you into getting the extra fries.

Kind of like Starbucks' protein, cheese, and cracker packs, which are just overpriced Lunchables for adults, your meal prep can become less painful by only prepping ingredients for the meals you would normally order.

For example, what would you order in a burrito bowl? Or a salad? I usually just choose my protein for the week, grill a ton of it, and then pick and choose various ingredients I can toss in a salad or pasta bowl (like an orzo) so I can switch it up and not hate myself by Tuesday. I won't bore you with recipes because there are literally millions of Pinterest ideas you can pore over while stoned at 2:00 in the morning, but generally buying a bunch of what you like and cutting up portions of it will win out over more time- and labor-intensive internet recipes. You can also make trying new recipes a Sunday night ritual, turning cooking into something you look forward to rather than dread—wine usually helps.

If you can't handle all five days sans purchased lunch (it does get pretty boring after a while), treat yourself to a bought lunch once a week. It'll be your reward for your hard work and "sacrifice" during the other four.

OFFICE ROMANCES

Ah, the tangled webs we weave for ourselves out of boredom, convenience, and total apathy for HR compliance. No matter how many people say it's not a good idea (and it's really, really not), you're still going to try and bang so-and-so from marketing because they're hot, they're there, and happy hour drinks were 2-for-1.

I can say from personal experience that an office romance is a *terrible* idea, especially if you're at different levels within the company. Fighting in meetings becomes a lot more vicious, if not more fun to watch for others.

Aside from making it awkward for your other coworkers, and even more painful for you to be in the office, it's just not a good look. Also, seeing the person you had a regrettable one-night stand with, or having to deal with the person that broke your heart every damn day, is inherently masochistic.

That being said, you're going to do it anyway—so just make sure HR has no hard and fast rules about dating coworkers and enjoy your terrible decisions while they last. Hey, whatever makes you more excited to get up and get dressed for work in the morning...

Can't wait to mourn my lost youth with back-to-school shopping for my office job.

FREELANCE VS. FULL-TIME

Most full-time roles offer important things, like paid time off, sick days, healthcare, commuting benefits, and retirement plans—also, you know, more job security. The trade-off is that you're working for this one company, rather than taking on a bunch of individual clients, working on your own schedule, and having the freedom to pick and choose who you work for at what time.

While many of us daydream of leaving the full-time rat race, some people are actually able to successfully jettison out.

Freelance writer Dave Infante lays out his reasoning for leaving his full-time gig:

"After eight years as a salaried writer with health benefits, I decided to become a freelancer. I wanted to do cooler stories that mattered more to more people, which I have to imagine is the leading cause for making such an abjectly aspirational decision. Also I don't have kids or a mortgage and it seemed like if I was ever going to do this, it was going to have to be right about now. Anyway, I've been at it for a few months now. I have not missed rent, I bought my own health insurance, and I continue eating and drinking at my standard (gluttonous) pace, so I guess things are going OK. The weirdest part of my new workday is the fact that it doesn't require me to speak with anyone. I just sit in my apartment, respond to emails, and try not to starve or injure myself. It's like the urban millennial version of *Hatchet*. (I'd love to tell that joke out loud but there's no one here to hear it.)"

As someone who has worked both as a full-time employee and as a contract worker, I think a successful freelancer is heavily dependent on having a strong network. If you have that network, have at it! If not, work full-time until you think you can secure it, or just keep working full-time and take on additional freelance gigs for extra cash.

"New year, new you," he said to his Chinese lunch special. General Tso remained silent.

ENTREPRENEURIALISM

Are you dead set on starting your own company? Does your idea for a business or brand keep you up at night? Are you willing to give up the cushion of working for someone else and getting a set, secure paycheck to pursue your dreams of being your own boss and creating cool shit? Then maybe being an entrepreneur is the right fit for you.

Because of freelance culture and the gig economy, there's a lot of opportunity to test out your entrepreneurial spirit on the side before you determine you feel comfortable flying solo (or with business partners).

I asked three entrepreneurs and business owners, all in their twenties, about their experiences becoming their own bosses. It's definitely not for the faint of heart:

- **Jack Carlson**, author, archaeologist, and founder of Rowing Blazers
- **Molly Borman**, founder of Just Nips Fake Nipples

• **Jared Greenman**, founder of @versus_brand and Yellow Cote Productions

What do you wish you had known about being an entrepreneur before you started your company?

JC: I wish I knew that you can't say yes to everything. When you're starting something new, and especially when you start to get some traction, people will come out of the woodwork. People you know, people you used to know, people you've never met but nevertheless give you a bro-hug and call you by your nickname—they'll all come out of the woodwork. They'll want to "pick your brain;" do a "collab;" grab a coffee; introduce you to a friend of theirs who has a great app that could really help a business like yours; connect you with their buddy who has some months experience doing something tangentially related to what you might eventually do. They want to invest but only on the most convoluted terms possible. Their cousin's band wants to write some music for you (what?). They want to be an influencer which means they want free things. They want to get on payroll as a consultant because, hey, you were in *The New York Times* once and now that means you must be made of money. They have this great opportunity for you to do an event in Tulsa, Oklahoma. They have an idea for you, which is how they would do your company completely differently if they were running it! But you can't say "yes" to all these things. In fact you can't say yes to basically any of them. It's hard to be a nice guy who keeps all these random people happy and run your business at the same time.

What are some of the largest challenges surrounding entrepreneurship?

JC: The relentlessness of it all. The sheer no-rest "Flying Dutchman" non-stopness of it. No matter where you are, no matter what you're doing, or however firmly you've managed to wrestle away a few minutes of respite, or, *mirabile dictu*, a few days of vacation—you will inevitably be blindsided by some unforeseen, urgent issue that you (and only you) can and must solve. A server is down. A form has to be filled out. A shipment is held up in customs at JFK Airport and only the authorized person (you) can go pick it up. Oh and make sure you bring a check for $8842.16 because that's the import tax that is owed because they changed the law last week. A celebrity wants to wear one of your things at his concert but he needs it hand-delivered from New York to this address in New Mexico by 3:00 pm today! The factory owner is having a mid-life crisis and you need to talk them back off the ledge. All three of your biggest accounts are at least six weeks late in paying you. UPS lost your package, for the ninth time this week. You got some great press, but now you have a stalker and they are *in your lobby*. A company in China has started knocking off your stuff, which reminds you—did you file that Chinese trademark paperwork?

MB: When I started Just Nips Fake Nipples, I wish I had known how much backlash we would get from stuffy, old white men who didn't understand the value of fake nipples and, by extension, female empowerment. Just kidding! I knew all that. That's one of the reasons I started Just Nips in the first place. But really, once I got through the idea phase and the fun creative design work, I suddenly had all these business-y things on my plate and I was like, *what?* Entrepreneurship is supposed to be picture-perfect for Instagram, right? Wrong.

Tax mumbo jumbo and legal jargon became my day-to-day and it was torture. *Where did all the fun go?* Ultimately, once I got through my first tax season, a bunch of payroll drama, and supply-chain logistics, the fun came back and I learned a ton about various operational tasks that make me sound very informed and even Harvard-esque to my peers.

JG: It's harder to sustain a business than to start one. Thanks to cheap online legal tools that help you incorporate (LegalZoom), easy access to manufacturers around the world (AliBaba), and an abundance of freelancers willing to create a logo for you on spec (Fiverr), it's really not that hard to start a business today. However, the goal isn't just to start a business so you can tell your friends and call yourself an entrepreneur, but rather to build something that grows and lasts. In order for that to happen, you need to get over the initial hump period where you might not see any traction, sales, user engagement, followers, etc. Figure out what's sticking and what's not and roll with what is. If your gut tells you it's a good idea, follow through long-term until you get your break.

I've started businesses that sell physical goods (art prints) and ones that don't (producing movies), and I wish I had known how important relationships were to success. Whether I was trying to land key talent or ask for pricing breaks from a vendor, the only way I found our enterprise getting ahead was by building strong personal ties with the key stakeholders that called that shots. For example, with @versus_brand I offered to do a video testimonial to help the owner promote his printing and framing business. The next day he offered to discount all my goods by 10% moving forward. Take the time to get to know the people you are dealing with and it will pay off.

Two of the largest challenges surrounding entrepreneurship are sales, and standing out from the crowd. No one thinks your idea is as good as you think it is. Unless you're willing to pound the pavement, pick up the phone, and knock out cold emails like Mike Tyson, that piggy bank won't be oinking on its own. You can make your life and chances at success easier if you think outside the box and create a business with a buzz/viral-worthy factor. Those type of ideas sometimes sell themselves...but only to a degree. Put your used-car-salesman shoes on and sell, baby, sell.

UNISEX WORK STAPLES

Every office has its own dress code, but it's not a bad idea to have a few staples at the ready that you can pair with more casual pieces or to have on-hand for interviewing. It doesn't get more obnoxious than shelling out a ton of dough on a stuffy suit you hate because you need it for that last-minute interview.

WHERE TO SHOP FOR OFFICE CLOTHES

I love Brooks Brothers' navy blazers because they can go through hell and back and still look great. And if you're a smaller girl, the boys' blazers are considerably less expensive and share the same quality. I've had mine for six years now and, while it wasn't cheap (~$200), it was definitely worth it.

Similarly, brands like J. McLaughlin and J. Crew have great work clothes that can transition to weekend wear. Finding new ways to slut up my office wardrobe is more of a lifestyle than a hobby for me.

Guy or girl, you should have some of the following:

- Navy and gray suit (black suits are for funerals). Girls don't necessarily need a full suit but blazers and trousers they can mix and match with.

- White button-down. As soon as it gets the yellow pits (that even OxiClean can't save), toss it.

- Good work shoes, like loafers.

- Your lucky interview accessory.
  For dudes it could be your favorite tie; for girls a stellar scarf, bag, or piece of jewelry.

- A solid work bag or padfolio.
  I recommend both, as showing up with a sweet padfolio to a meeting or interview is such a power move.

Regarding your work bag, you're going to use it every day and people will notice it, so it should be an investment piece rather than one of the million free canvas totes littering your hallway closet. I use and love a Filson tote for work purposes and also as a smaller overnight bag in a pinch, but you should find something you're similarly enamored with that can fit all the odds and ends, and potentially a lunch bag.

I'm alternately disgusted and impressed by the number of shoes I own.

CHAPTER 4

Dating

Will you still love me when I'm no longer young and tolerant of your substance abuse?

Navigating the constantly evolving modern dating scene is a struggle, to say the least. How we date and where we predominantly meet one another may have changed, but our primal urges and emotional needs irrevocably stay the same—at least until they perfect sex robots and the nerds really take over.

Gone are the days of assuming you'll ride out eternity with the people you grew up with or met in school.* We're living longer and putting off kids until we've "found" ourselves and our careers.

According to a 2018 Goldman Sachs study, the median age for marriage in the U.S. is currently 30 years old, compared to 23 in the 1970s. It's a wide world out there, and all the limitless possibilities that come with the internet make it easier to question monogamy. The real question is, how do you play all this to your advantage with the fewest possible hurt feelings?

*By no means am I bashing ending up with your high school or college sweetheart (Hi, Mom and Dad!). That turn of events is often preferable, but the majority of this chapter will be catered towards people who haven't found their ideal partner yet.

APPS

The advent of dating apps is a new form of digital Darwinism; only the strongest profiles get the most matches.

As time marches on, it seems like there's a new app every other month that caters to another personal preference. Similar geographical location is obvious, but you can also filter based on religion, sexuality, preferred kink, profession, and race. A lot of the latter choices might seem like not-very-progressive or indeed dickish moves, but those stringently limiting their choices end up doing everyone else a favor by taking themselves out of the dating pool.

Unfortunately, the sheer number of available apps is a double-edged sword, because many users will download all of the popular ones in their area to avoid FOMO. You'll see the same people on the apps over and over again (like the cyclical pattern of abuse that is dating). The other downside to having so many dating apps is spending precious time communicating with the various people you meet on them. Many of the conversations will turn out to be dead ends, but it's important to discern whether you actually want to meet up with the person or save yourself an awkward two hours you'll never get back.

But at the end of the long and emotionally draining day, dating apps are an incredible way to meet a larger group of people you may never have encountered. Or perhaps you would have eventually, but this little darling piece of tech speeds up the process. By having the opportunity to date more, you learn more about what you like and don't like in other people, which is an excellent and often overlooked exercise in itself. You don't know for certain that you like or detest something until you try it—so give yourself and other people the benefit of the doubt. More often than not, you'll be glad you did.

Even if you're not sold on the concept of apps, it's not a bad idea to download one if you're looking to meet people in a new city.

CONSTRUCTING YOUR APP PROFILE—TIPS AND TRICKS

A good app profile will display how multifaceted you are by showing

> # I hope someone is creating a dating app for carpenters and construction workers called Stud Finder.

pictures or videos of yourself in interesting places while simultaneously highlighting (legal) activities you enjoy. Whether that's day drinking, tennis, or volunteering with various teacup-sized rescue animals—you do you.

Your best picture should go first, because people tend to swipe right or left at the first feeling of "nah" or "ooooh." An "ooooh" or "meh" warrants swiping towards more photos where you can show off even more (literally and figuratively) through the magic of good lighting and friends with photography skills. A selection of four or five good photos with a maximum of one selfie should do.

Group shots are a solid addition if only because everyone feels this need to prove they have friends (congratulations on that, by the way). But, if it's all group shots, expect people to swipe left out of apathy concerning the amount of time it'll take to figure out which person you are.

"No, you can't join Farmers Only because you're tired of paying for organic produce."

Other photos you should be wary of, unless you're intentionally trying to weed people out, include:

- Gun photos
- Photos in front of luxury items
- Selfies
- Selfies with blatant filters on them
- Photos of you with a sedated tiger
- Seriously obnoxious sorority/fraternity/bachelor/bachelorette party photos
- Your blatant LinkedIn profile photo
- Baby photos
- Multiple photos of you with babies
- Photos where you look terrible but you took a selfie with a celebrity so—YOLO
- Photos that show your political affiliation
- Photo with an ex that includes their face angrily scribbled out
- Nudes

If you're including video clips, chugging any sort of alcohol or ripping a cig or vape is discouraged—because you'll look like an idiot.

Now that you've assembled mixed media that showcases your stunning good looks and vibrant lifestyle, it's time for the bio.

If it's the question and answer format, remember to keep it short, witty, and grammatically correct. It's also in your best interest to remain truthful, so it's not false advertising and you don't attract the wrong people. For example, if you say you love camping and the very idea of sleeping outside makes you shiver with contempt, don't lie so you can snag a Patagonia-wearing hottie. There are enough startup founders who can fulfill that faux granola fantasy.

If it's a blank slate you can fill at your own discretion, try to keep it short, sweet, and memorable. Two to three sentences, max. No one wants to read a novel about you before they know if you've even matched.

APPS IN CITIES VS. SUBURBS

There are pros and cons to being on apps in bustling cities versus rural areas. Cities have the luxury of *choice*: like a highly caloric array of cakes you can't have too much of or you'll lose your appetite altogether. This illusion of unending choice leads to people perpetually thinking they can do better than their current partner, or multiple partners, and there's also the issue of dating fatigue.

From personal experience I can tell you dating in a city gets tiring. You really have to put in the work, and you don't know right off the bat if someone is interested in dating you to see if there's relationship potential, or if they just want to see you naked and peace shortly after. However, things always seem to work out, even in the city that never sleeps, or never stops sleeping around, and I have plenty of friends that have met the love of their life through app dating.

I asked my friend Brian, a Jersey suburbs native, about his experience with app dating outside the city, and it seems he had a similar experience:

"Dating in the suburbs isn't as difficult as it seems—but you have to get creative. The trick is to expand your search parameters to include the nearest big city. I live only 12 miles or so from Manhattan, so the dating pool is similar to the city. There have been a few instances where

"Breakfast for dinner!" she ecstatically yelled to her empty apartment. A drug dealer loitering on the street heard her shrill announcement through the open window and nodded in approval.

matches didn't respond when they heard where I lived. But people in the city are fickle...they would be equally as dismissive if I lived in Brooklyn or even in downtown Manhattan. Some people are looking right in their neighborhood."

Leah, a friend that moved from Manhattan to Kentucky for grad school, has had a vastly different experience:

"Dating apps outside of major cities is like going to an all-you-can-eat buffet at a questionable restaurant. There's always going to be a lot of choices, but you really have to dig around to find the dishes that won't make you feel ill after a few hours. I'm not thrilled with the selection I have and I know everyone feels the same way about their own city or town, but it's *unreal* here. I've had more interesting conversations with patrons half conscious at last call than with men from rural Kentucky on Tinder."

> # "The beginning of our love story is like a modern day *The Notebook*."
>
> # "Didn't he DM you nudes?"

SENDING AND RECEIVING NUDES

There is an ambiguous etiquette to sending nudes. You don't want to jump the gun with a full-blown crotch shot unless it's explicitly asked for, or you feel like the other party *really* wants it (and guys—she rarely wants your dick pic unless she asks for it).

If you feel comfortable enough to send the other party a celebration of your body then great, all the power to you. Self-confidence is a beautiful, magnetic, and underappreciated thing, especially with good lighting. And you might as well capture it while you still have some semblance of a metabolism.

The downside to sending nudes is (obviously) the high potential of them getting shared. The recipient could immediately be saving the photo and sending it to a large group chat to be discussed in detail; or they could be doing nothing with it. It depends on the person and their ulterior motives/penchant for blackmailing.

But remember—life is too short. If you're dating the person and you want to send nudes, send a damn nude. Just be aware of the potential consequences, keep your face out of photos, and depending on your profession, you may really, really need to keep it in your pants.

"Sometimes I wonder if the effort spent on my nighttime skincare routine is worth it. But eventually, I'll look back and say, 'Hey, at least I tried.'"

Their date: "I just asked if you've seen any good movies recently."

PAYING FOR DATES

Who pays for the dates is a gray area that is a "damned if you do, damned if you don't" scenario. If it's a hetero couple, women do get paid $.79 on the dollar, so it's not the *worst* for the guy to pay for the first date. This screws hetero men over if they're perpetually going on first dates, but it's the gentlemanly thing to do. Women should at least offer, physically pull out their wallet to split, and be ready to go through with it if he takes you up on your offer. If they decline your offer and pay, be sure to thank them after the fact.

My hetero friends go back and forth on who should pay—another option is whomever did the asking out should purchase the drinks or meal. If someone is asking you out and wants a recommendation, only suggest a place that you personally would feel comfortable paying for or splitting. Even if you assume you won't pay, don't suggest an exorbitantly priced place, a) because it's the decent thing to do, and, b) in case you end up footing the bill.

I asked James Perry Adams, a public affairs consultant in Washington, D.C. what the protocol is for paying on dates between members of the same sex:

> "One of the many wonderful things about being a gay man in the modern era is not needing to subscribe to antiquated hetero-patriarchal norms that only further gender inequality. When two men are on a date, my preference, and the preference of most guys I know, is to split the bill down the middle. It's quick and easy. It keeps things equal. It doesn't create a power dynamic or expectation for further activities later on."

Regardless of gender or sexual orientation, after the first date both parties should split the bill or alternate paying to make things more equal. If one person in the relationship/thing/consequence-of-societal-pressures is getting paid a lot more than the other, it's an unspoken rule that they're picking up the bill more often.

But that's for you two to fight over on your own time.

EXES

Ah, the Sisyphean burden of lost love. Or mutual apathy. Whatever your relationship with your ex is, please be aware that your mental health should always come first.

Depending on how things end, presumably without someone's stuff getting set on fire, it's natural to want to speak or hang out with them again. Especially after being thrust into the cruel reality that is dating. Or going through a dry spell. Or realizing that you'll actually have to try and make a new person like you, which is totally fine in theory but tiring in practice.

Do they have spa packages for when your ex gets engaged?

To keep the peace with them—but more importantly, yourself—abide by these few cardinal rules of a recent break-up.

SPACE

This is one of the most blindingly apparent, yet disturbingly hardest things to do when you first call it quits. Do not talk to them. Do not see them. I cannot stress that enough. It isn't an effective decision if one or both of you is constantly harassing the other or texting in the middle of the night. You can't just turn your feelings off and on like a light (and this is a good thing because it proves you're not a sociopath). Sticking to your "no contact whatsoever" regimen is going to suck but it *will* get better over time, and you'll thank yourself in a few months.

SPLITTING UP FRIENDS

The dividing of your friends can either be an incredibly easy or impossibly difficult task. You clearly came into the relationship with your respective friends, but they could also have become attached to your significant other and vice versa.

It's different in every situation but, at the end of the day, go with your gut and stay friends with whomever you want. It's a free country and this was a break-up, not a diplomatic mission. Conversely, don't force your friends to choose sides or pressure them into never speaking to or seeing the other person again. That's not your choice to make for them and they'll resent you for it.

PUBLIC SHIT-TALKING

First of all, you're better than this. In a world of social media and screen-grabbing, publicly shit-talking the person who used to see you naked is a huge no-no. It just comes off as catty and unhinged, which you might actually be, but shouldn't broadcast now that you're single.

The same goes for word-of-mouth. Don't say anything you wouldn't want to get back to your ex, and remember that people won't look at you as a mature person worthy of respect if you're airing the dirty laundry of someone you used to truly care about. Also, your ex could just as easily retaliate. Play it cool as much as you humanly can, and complain to your friends and/or therapist in confidence.

SLEEPING WITH THEIR FRIENDS

Not a great idea! If you're trying to get back at your ex, this will not only make you look terrible, but can hurt a lot more feelings during an already toxic time.

Plus, it's only effective if their friend is a lot more attractive than your ex. Not just marginally more attractive, but like a full grade higher than them. The only way you can get away with banging someone slightly more attractive than them is if they're exponentially more successful. Pick your battles (or their former college roommates) wisely.

GHOSTING

Ghosting, or simply disappearing on the person you were seeing, has become a trademark of our generation. It's not like we're excelling in in-person communication anyway—not answering texts feels like a less painful way to exit the situation than having the trite, "It's not you, it's me" talk.

Like everything in life, there are pros and cons to ghosting, and it depends on the situation.

Pro: Avoiding the conversation/insipid excuse about why you two aren't working out.
Con: No closure and leaves them hanging. It's also a sign of a lack of maturity.

If you have been seeing the other person for more than two dates, then ghosting is out of the question. A phone call or text loosely along the lines of, "Hey,

Social media is great for checking in on people you never wanted to see again.

it was great to meet you but I don't think this is going to work out. Wish you all the best," is deserved.

If it's been one or two dates and you're not feeling it and the other person isn't texting you either, congrats! *You've successfully ghosted each other without confrontation.* That's completely acceptable ghosting, and only viable if the other person isn't trying to get in touch with you either. That's the great thing about chemistry, it's usually apparent or not and both of you can respectively, silently acknowledge the lack of a future together and move on.

I asked my exceptionally polite friend Spencer Hughes about his thoughts on ghosting, and wasn't surprised that he doesn't practice it but, "I understand if my date does it to me. The writing was probably on the wall so it's not that surprising if it happens. However, it's appropriate for either party to close the loop if things aren't going to work."

If someone's texted you twice and you've neglected to respond then it's acknowledged that you ghosted them (which isn't very nice). If they continue to text and try and get in contact with you, then kindly let them know this isn't working out.

The same goes for you—if you double-texted and they haven't responded, there's a good chance they're on their way out, which brings us to...

It's exhausting having this many feelings.

SLOW-FADING

Slow-fading is when the person you're seeing is slowly withdrawing from your life. Not enough to cause immediate alarm, but you have adequate reason or a gut feeling that something's up. Maybe their text response time has doubled, tripled, or just dissipated altogether. Maybe they're not as gung ho about plans or have stopped making them. Maybe they've stopped sending you funny memes, which is the cruelest sign of all.

All of these signals could mean the other person is considering leaving the relationship and, rather than dump you outright, wants to make you dislike them enough that you'll withdraw as well or dump them instead. It's a total cop-out in place of saying how they really feel, and definitely the path of least resistance for them.

If you're doing this to another person, even inadvertently, take a good hard look at your actions and decide if you want to be instigating mind games. It sucked when others did it to you; don't perpetuate this cycle of mental anguish and instead make an actionable decision that doesn't involve hoping the other person (who *likes you*) takes a hint.

BENCHING

Benching is a fairly new phenomenon, made possible through the joys of texting and social media. It's when you're put on the "bench," with potential to be put back in the game. The person benching you isn't sure if they want to hang out again, but definitely wants the luxury of keeping the possibility alive—either because their own ego demands that they have the most number of people available at their beck and call, or they can't see themselves with you now, but who knows if and when their mind will change.

Unlike ghosting you don't completely disappear, but remain on the periphery, sporadically reminding the other person of your existence, either by liking posts, texting every few weeks or months, or always watching their social media posts even when you know it's visible to them.

Based off the many, many conversations I've had with friends about benching, it's either a somewhat malicious endeavor, because the other person still has a selfish desire to see what you're up to, or they're actually oblivious to what they're doing to your mental state.

They don't really qualify as the one that got away if they still "like" all your Instagram posts.

For instance, after getting slow-faded, ghosted, and then dumped after I demanded an explanation from a guy I was seeing, he continued to bench me. I was livid because he didn't unfollow me from social media, and continued to like or view all of my posts. He replied that he just wanted to see how I was doing, and honestly didn't mean to continuously torture me with notifications. He's an idiot but I trust him. Don't be like that guy, and unfollow the people you were seeing so they can't see you lurking, innocently or not.

SHOULD YOU GOOGLE YOUR DATE BEFORE MEETING THEM?

Googling your date before actually meeting up is almost a given now. With a disturbing amount of information available within seconds, why not do some reconnaissance to see if the person you've only chatted with sparingly and know mostly from photos is a registered sex offender?

While that's a glaringly obvious red flag, I've trained myself to take online presences with a grain of salt because I know mine isn't the most, um...

"She considers herself a lifestyle brand & refers to her Instagram as a foodie blog."
"Say no more."

pristine. My personal and parody Twitter accounts, articles I've written about dating, regrettable videos of me reporting and eating mass quantities of stunt food on camera...it never ends. I'm not surprised when guys ghost me after we've set a tentative date, I just assume they looked me up online and weren't thrilled with what they saw.

Once an ex brought up my "dating a doctor for prescription access" jokes from my parody account on our second date. They were older jokes but the medical student was still genuinely concerned I was seeing him for the wrong reasons. Sure, I should have seen the writing on the wall when he couldn't discern that it was a parody, but I appreciated his candor in admitting what he found online bothered him without just immediately writing me off. Because of his maturity, I was able to explain myself and we ended up seeing each other for a few more months before it completely crashed and burned.

"He has so many layers, like a slutty onion."

I asked the author, stand-up comedian, and genius behind @NYTVows, Selena Coppock, about her feelings on Googling before dates and she was also a fan of the practice:

> "I always Google before a first date, but I think it's a very stupid move on my part, because I'm not a good actress. Years back, before a first date, I looked up the guy online and found that he was a former gym teacher who had been arrested for drug dealing (yikes!) and lost his job. I went on the first date with him (hey, ya never know, people change) and on that first date, this handsome, heavily tattooed hottie 'revealed' to me that he had lost his teaching job because he was arrested for selling drugs. I had to act surprised by this news and pretend to be *just* learning this information. I'm not a strong enough actress to pull that off. It was very tricky. So if you're going to Google, be sure to sign up for acting classes."

SHOULD YOU MOVE IN TOGETHER?

Ah yes, the complicated question of when it's appropriate to move in together. You've reached the point in your relationship where you're:

- Already cohabitating in theory, because lying around without pants together is a staple of your relationship.

- You only go home to pick up office-appropriate clothes so your coworkers don't think you've become a vagrant.

- Any roommates probably aren't thrilled with your significant other's constant presence and taking up valuable bathroom counter real estate.

- You've been dating long enough that you feel comfortable taking the jump to sharing a bathroom. And that's a big jump.

How many throw pillows does it take to fill the void?

SO, WHAT'S THE HOLDUP?

Part-emotional, part-financial, and highly problematic, moving in together is often a make-or-break scenario for many relationships. Money and financial issues are among some of the top reasons why marriages fail, and the same can be said for relationships when you're shouldering living costs together. But hey, it's better to realize your partner isn't the right fit before any owned property or kids are involved.

Rent should be 28% of your combined income, and how you split that is up to you. This is the first hurdle to get over, because you and your SO may not be facing the same financial pressures. One of you may be making more money, the other may have massive student loans; one is still getting money from their parents, one owes a massive amount to their fantasy football team—the list goes on and on.

PAYING BILLS WHEN YOU'RE SHARING EXPENSES

If you're already worried about reminding them to pay their share of the living expenses, you can make it more seamless by setting up a direct deposit into a separate, joint checking account that's for rent, utilities, and groceries. This way you'll have a set amount going in each month and there's less money actively changing hands. More importantly, you won't have to constantly remind each other to pay the damn bills.

SPLITTING UP UTILITIES

Companies will need to speak to the person whose name is on the bill to settle billing and service disputes—having your name listed on the account won't always work. Split up who's taking care of what utility so one person isn't shouldered with every account and customer service nightmare.

GIFT EXPERIENCES RATHER THAN THINGS

To make gifts easier on one another (like oh, cool, we can't afford a vacation but you thought I'd want this travel kit?), choose something that you can enjoy together instead of letting an item collect dust in the closet. Meals, vacations, museum trips, or concerts are something you can make a memory with and are less likely to spark contention. Unless they really wanted *that thing* they've been *hinting at* all year—then that's on you, buddy.

BEING SINGLE IS COOL

I'm not here to give you a half-hearted pep talk about how being alone is the bees knees while sullenly staring out the window and swiping on Tinder. Being single is great. You wake up alone, make your own coffee the way you like it, choose what you want to eat or where and with whom, and don't have to constantly worry if the minutiae of your day is affecting someone else. Making decisions for one is unfathomably easier than taking someone else's whole life into account. You can do whatever you want, when you want,

> "Self-care Saturday!" she yelled, cracking open a Bud Light in the middle of the autumnal farmers market.

without pissing off a partner who has to work early the next morning and really hates your taste in reality TV.

Does it get lonely? Sometimes—you see your friends with their partners and think, "Awww, I want someone to do light PDA with." However, you should choose to be in a relationship because you want to be with that particular person you can't get enough of, not because of the social stigma against the uncoupled.

Choose freedom until there's someone worth giving it up for! Live for yourself and grow into a person that won't lose their identity in a relationship! Enjoying your own company is one of the most valuable skills you can learn. Plus, you get to hook up with whomever you want.

TEMPERING YOUR EXPECTATIONS

Hannah Orenstein, dating editor at *Elite Daily* and author of the novel *Playing With Matches* (Touchstone, 2018), is a former matchmaker at a top dating service, and I was interested in hearing about the most prevalent issue she had setting up clients. Of course it was the laundry list of qualities that the person wanted in a partner:

> "One client literally gave me a six-page checklist, and after every date I sent her on, she would email an annotated checklist back to me to explain where I had failed to meet her expectations. I completely understand why people have checklists—you're amazing, you deserve someone equally amazing. It's easy to get caught up in wanting a person who looks perfect on paper. But the truth is that you're ultimately going to meet someone who's incredible for you in ways that you can't possibly predict."

"Why are you dressed in tennis whites when you don't play."

"I wanted to advertise that I'm pure."

When asked about the key to finding a successful relationship, Hannah suggested, "Keep an open mind, go out with a lot of people, and see who you click with. If you have to have a checklist, keep it short and focused primarily on non-superficial traits."

FRIENDS WITH BENEFITS

We all have those friends you find attractive but definitely wouldn't date because you know too much about them. Sometimes the stars align and you

The only time I wish I had a boyfriend is when I'm trying and failing to put on a fitted sheet.

find out they feel similarly (usually alcohol is involved), and you manage to finagle a friends-with-benefits scenario.

In a perfect world, this is a situation where you get sex without any of the emotional roadblocks in the way. But usually it starts because one friend actually likes the other and is hoping for an ending worthy of a romantic comedy. Or, you both just want to have sex. If it's the latter, good for you!

This is possible if:

- You're both (sincerely) not interested in dating one another
- You're respectful of one another and your friendship
- Neither party is getting emotionally hurt by this

Eventually, because feelings are a tricky beast, it's not unusual for at least one person in the coming weeks or months to question if they're in this for the right reasons. Continuously check up with each other and keep asking if this is getting weird, and if so, it's time to cool it. Getting off occasionally isn't worth losing a friendship. Besides, if you want emotionless sex, that's what your exes are for!

There's a ratio for how hot you are versus how much bullshit you're allowed to get away with. EX SEX

Like friends with benefits, there are a few things you have to ask yourself before showing up at 2:00 a.m. with Taco Bell in lieu of flowers. Are you doing this purely for physical reasons? Are you still emotionally attached to them? Are you going through with this because you're still holding out hope?

If you can honestly tell yourself that you're mostly devoid of feelings for them and this is just to maintain your sanity or so you don't hook up with strangers, then no judgments here!

No, you can't start a charity for your eskimo sisters because they "clearly need help."

However, if it seems that your ex is doing this as an attempt to get back into your life and favor, then be kind and don't give them that futile hope you'll get back together. There's something to be said about treating others like you'd like to be treated, even if their fashion sense, breath, and decor is horrible.

IT'S PERFECTLY FINE NOT TO SLEEP AROUND

In our sex-positive environment, we've been trained to tell ourselves that it's okay to sleep around as long as you're safe and no one gets hurt. But what if you are? What if you can't have one night stands without feeling disgusting? What if you don't want to hook up with your ex because it's emotionally damaging? What if you're holding out for the right person? You know what? Good for you.

Stick to your guns and try to not feel pressured by your more "outgoing" friends and dates. Only you know what you're comfortable with and there's zero reason to try and live by someone else's expectations of you.

HOW TO DUMP SOMEONE

In short, don't sugarcoat it. Dancing around the actual act of dumping someone by complimenting them, telling them how great they are, and why you care about them is making the act easier on you—not them.

A 2017 Pew Research Center study concluded that most people want the Band-Aid ripped off when it comes to bad news, and suggested you start the conversation with some of the most hated words in the English language: "We need to talk." This way the other party knows what's coming and can emotionally brace themselves. No one likes being rejected; don't be the schmuck that drags it out for as long as humanly possible like a car wreck in slow motion. Yes, it will feel weird not going into a whole spiel about how much you appreciate them, but it's much kinder to just buffer it slightly and then get it over with.

9/10 doctors agree it's for the best for you to stop texting me.

WHEN IT'S ACCEPTABLE TO BREAK UP OVER TEXT OR EMAIL

You may think it's incredibly rude or improper to break up with someone over text or email but, depending on how you or they handle certain situations, you might be doing them a favor. It's not the coward's way out to put it in writing or over the phone if:

- **You feel like you're going to screw it up in person**
  Do you suck in stressful situations? Will you do a lot of the aforementioned sugarcoating of the news, or will your not wanting to make them upset lead to you not actually breaking up? Then putting it in writing or over the phone may be best.

- **You know they're going to drag it out as long as possible**
  If they're going to launch into a million reasons why you should stay together, and continue needing closure, don't put either of you through the most exhausting three hour-coffee date of your life.

- **They're not going to accept it**
  If they can't accept the fact that you no longer want to see them, doing it bluntly and in a finite manner will help them process what's going on. They may think you're a dick, but at least they'll know it's definitely over.

"Why did he dump you?"

"I got wasted and wouldn't stop yelling 'play 'Freebird'" at his stupid indie jam band concert."

GETTING BROKEN UP WITH

There's no way around it; getting broken up with sucks. You've been rejected by one of the people you care about most, and it's going to sting for a while. Days, months, years—however long the relationship was, it will have a complementary window of mourning time. They were an integral part of your life and it's now over, there's no use in undermining that amount of pain.

You're allowed to wallow in your own misery, and maybe even go on a bender if it'll help you get it out of your system and move on. The important thing is giving yourself time to grieve, accept the loss and *eventually* meet other people who will acknowledge how fucking fantastic you are. Don't just jump on the dating bandwagon, allow yourself some alone time—and don't use other people (physically or emotionally) as a temporary Band-Aid for your own troubles.

Another thing to accept is that you weren't broken up with out of malice or spite. People are looking for specific things in others and if you don't have an exact trait or lifestyle choice the other person is looking for, that may be their deal breaker. That you're lacking the random feature they're adamant about doesn't make you any less of a person, but, by all means, you're still allowed to be pissed off about the situation.

Who needs a hobby when you can blatant-ly abuse the internet for your own gain?

DON'T LEAD PEOPLE ON IF YOU'RE NOT INTERESTED

If someone's really into you but you're not feeling it, don't lead them on just because you enjoy the attention or validation that comes with someone having a crush on you. That's what posting thirst-traps on social media are for.

Even if you think you're just being nice by not explicitly turning them down, don't let them keep holding onto unnecessary hope that you'll come around. It's not fair or nice and they already like you; put them down gently and be done with it.

DON'T TALK INCESSANTLY ABOUT YOUR S.O.

Your friends can put up with a lot, but not your constant chatter about what your significant other (S.O.) is up to. They didn't pay for overpriced brunch drinks to hear about what your boo is doing at their parents' house this weekend. In fact, that report could not be any less interesting.

Keep reminding yourself that no one else is going to find their biting commentary on Netflix true-crime documentaries as enrapturing as you do. You're enamored with them and ignoring how tedious you sound because that new-crush feeling hasn't worn off.

"She said she was dating a doctor."
"Perpetually keeping a tab open on Web-MD doesn't count."

He just posted Cancun pics with the caption, "baecation." He's dead to me.

On a similar note, don't be too disturbingly happy in front of everyone, both in-person with your friends or on social media. Others may be going through a rough patch, feeling particularly lonely, or downright pissed off, and your exceptional good fortune is going to make them feel like shit and maybe not root for your relationship to succeed. Especially if you're punning in your Instagram captions while wearing matching outfits.

"I'm sorry our couples' Halloween costume triggered you."

"Marilyn Monroe with both RFK and JFK was a little much."

Learn to temper your happiness on the outside, but feel free to be giddy as hell to yourself or the close friends that share in your happiness. Enjoy it! Revel in it! That feeling doesn't come along too often and should be rightfully appreciated.

DON'T DISAPPEAR ON YOUR FRIENDS 🚫

Your friends won't appreciate it if you up and ghost on them as soon as you get a new partner. Yes, you may be in the throes of new love and you can't imagine spending time apart, but someone who spends all their social time with one person quickly becomes burdensome. You need your friends, and your partner needs theirs.

Plus, what happens if you and the hero or heroine of the hour don't work out? Your friends won't look kindly on you crawling back after a long hiatus without thought for *their* feelings. In short, don't be the person that only has friendships when it's convenient for you.

THE BEST COUPLES ARE AS COOL TOGETHER AS THEY ARE APART

When I think of a good couple, I think of my friends Nick and Julia, because they're just as fun together as they are alone. They even planned their wedding while Julia was working in Australia for six months and Nick continued to work and live in NYC. I asked Julia how they managed to stay together even though they were a continent away and with old and new friends:

"I know it sounds trite, but: communicate *a lot*. I am extremely lucky in that Nick has an exceptionally high EQ and can see through me when I shut down and become passive-aggressive. Air your shit out. Talk about everything. Even if it's nonsensical, just say, 'I am feeling frustrated and upset and insecure and I don't know why so please be gentle with me today.' I often say, 'pay attention to me' when I am feeling vulnerable and, guess what? It works better than making Nick guess why I am being mean and cagey."

DON'T TREAT YOUR S.O. AS A STATUS SYMBOL

Welcome to the world of Instagram relationships, where touting a significant other like some sort of trophy is not only widely accepted, but encouraged.

Matching or complementary outfits, "heart eye" emojis, Drake song lyric captions...the extent to which people want to scream at the top of their lungs, "Look! Someone wants to be with me!" is deafening. There's a reason for this tendency to overshare; studies have shown that the more people post about their relationship, the more insecure they feel about it. It's as if they're not only proving it to the world, but to themselves as well. (Also bear in mind that influencers and bloggers make more money and get more gigs from brands as a couple rather than as a single person.)

More often than not, the ostentatious relationship #goals pics are staged...who doesn't want to look their best on social media? Don't scour the happy hour scene just looking for an Instagram prop, it never ends well.

DON'T TRY TO CHANGE PEOPLE

It's a simple concept and we're all guilty of doing it from time to time: trying to DIY someone into an idealized version who you'll like better. You have to grasp that they're not your biggest Pinterest project yet, but rather someone who thinks you've accepted them. I'm not talking about trying to fix their consistently leaving the toilet seat up or a tendency to get hairspray on every reflective surface (you should definitely harp on them for that), but larger goals that would affect the course of your life.

If you don't have similar long-term goals as your partner, it's not worth waiting around with the desperate, furtive hope you can make them change

"Why did you guys break up?"

"He wouldn't stop watching those tiny house shows and it terrified me."

Vanessa Carlton would walk 1,000 miles and you won't even do a subway transfer for me.

their mind. After an appropriate amount of time, having the difficult conversations about where you eventually see this going is always a good idea. It will be anxiety-inducing at first, but it's worth sitting down and having an honest discussion rather than letting it get more high-stakes as the relationship progresses.

Julia, part of the aforementioned golden couple I referred to earlier, chimed in with this:

"Talk about the future. It is much better for Nick to know now I don't want kids than for me to tell him once we're married. I am shocked by the number of people I know who got married and only then discovered they wanted to live in entirely different countries."

Stick to your priorities, respect your partner's, and acknowledge that if you have different visions of the future or can't at least compromise, it probably wasn't meant to be.

SIGNS THAT THE RELATIONSHIP IS OVER

While not all good things must necessarily come to an end, the lukewarm ones definitely do. Complacency is the death of any relationship, and the warning signs will be there, even if they're not obvious.

Respect the warning signs and either accept that this relationship is probably on its way out, or do a 180° and twist the narrative so things have a chance of improving.

THEY'RE NO LONGER PERFORMING FAVORS
Did they used to love to cook dinner as a sign of their affection but now just order Seamless? Used to wake you up with coffee but now tell you to make your own damn latte? Their feelings may be waning along with their enthusiasm for doing favors out of the goodness of their heart.

YOU'RE NOT TALKING ABOUT SEX AND JUST GOING THROUGH THE MOTIONS
If sex is getting mechanical and you're not exploring new options in favor of the old standbys, then sex has become less of a priority, which is a bad sign. Sex with your partner should be better than "whatever" or you'll start looking or imagining someone else with whom it could be better.

YOU'RE NOT TALKING A LOT IN GENERAL. MEALS ARE EATEN IN SILENCE, OR WHILE ON YOUR PHONES.
Not having a lot to say to one another is another egregious red flag (that

you might initially overlook if you think they're super hot). However, if you're already running out of things to talk about, what's going to happen when you're not physically attracted to them either?

THERE'S A LOT OF "SATURDAYS ARE FOR THE BOYS" OR "GIRLS' NIGHTS," NOT BECAUSE THEY MISS THEIR FRIENDS, BUT BECAUSE THEY WANT TIME OFF FROM YOU
Relationships are work and avoiding the work doesn't help.

THEY GET DEFENSIVE, NOT EMPATHETIC WHEN CONFRONTED
If they're throwing issues right back at you rather than acknowledging and then trying to find a solution during a fight, they're probably not happy either.

THEY'RE CHEATING ON YOUR JOINT NETFLIX SHOWS
It may seem silly but if they don't respect you enough to not cheat on your show routine, who knows what else they're doing without you?

YOU'RE BORED
If you're bored, you're unhappy. And if you're not happy then what's the point of being in this relationship when you can find someone else who *will* make you happy?

YOU'RE CONSIDERING CHEATING OR THEY ALREADY CHEATED
Welp. This one's a given. If you're looking elsewhere or they already have, decide if this is a relationship worth fighting for or if you're ready to throw in the towel. Acknowledging you're no longer right for each other is definitely a shitty exercise, but a very mature one and better than them walking in on you with your SoulCycle instructor.

Never trust a grown-ass man who wants to take you to Disneyland.

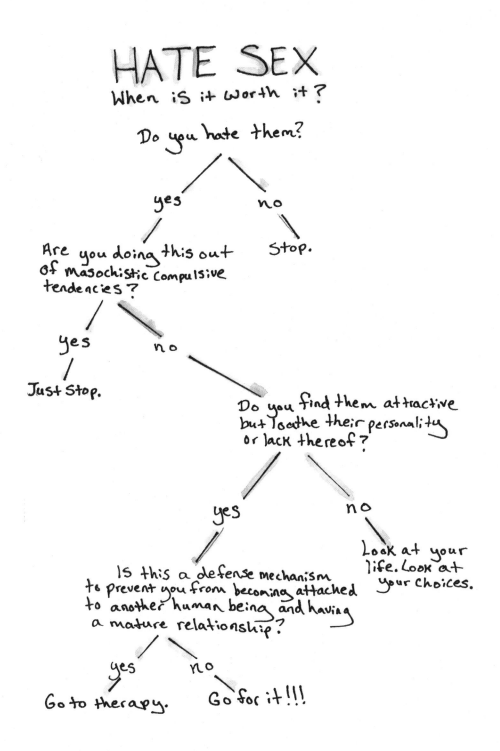

CHAPTER 5

Finances

Whenever you feel sad, remember how much potential blackmail is saved in your camera roll.

Whoever told you that money doesn't buy happiness is a shitty liar. Money buys healthcare, a place for you to live, decent food, the essentials, and all the extras you need to have fun and keep up a lifestyle you're comfortable with—which, more or less, equates to a foundation, or the higher potential, for happiness. Money just as importantly equates to freedom: the freedom to pursue a career you enjoy, live on your own terms, and not be stuck in relationships that you may have been forced to tolerate to save money.

Having money also cuts down on stress, and not in a, "Ugh, brunch is going to be $40" shallow passing concern. More of a "not panicking about the lights being turned off because you couldn't pay the electric bill," or "questioning if you're going to get scurvy from eating nothing but McDonald's and ramen for the last week."

As an adult, as excruciatingly painful as it may be, it's crucial to not only keep track of your finances and make a budget tailored to your lifestyle, but also to save for the future so you don't hate yourself down the line. Future You wants to retire and enjoy a life not tethered to Excel sheets and an open office plan where someone brought fish to microwave for lunch, yet again.

The good thing is, you're young. And even if you haven't started saving yet, there's no time like the present. I'm not a financial planner by any means, but I know the basics, and have watched my portfolio ebb and flow with the seasons and political strife. This is also a prime time to insert a self-deprecating-Jew joke, but I'll abstain.

Just FYI, this chapter is a simplification of seriously complicated matters and please do your own extensive research before investing. All percentages and business information, unless stated otherwise, have been sourced from TheStreet.com.

STOCK MARKET, EXPLAINED

Think of the stock market like smart gambling. It has its highs and lows and, unlike actual gambling, is highly encouraged, so you don't get screwed over by inflation. (Inflation is a rise in the price of goods and services that erodes the value of the dollar. Like how, without fail, your rent goes up every year, but you may not get a raise. That's why your money has to actively work for you—because otherwise it's decreasing in value.)

If you own a stock, you own a piece of a company, and you buy a piece of a company through the stock market. When people talk about the stock market, they're referring to all the stocks in general, not just the New York Stock Exchange (NYSE). You've probably seen the NYSE in movies; it's that big building with pillars on Wall Street and a big-ass American flag on it.

The "stock market" is a reference to all of the individual markets. For example there is the S&P 500, the Dow Jones Industrial Average, and the NASDAQ (tech stocks) composite. The indexes are an average of some of the more representative stocks that give you a sense of how the market is doing.

WAIT, SO HOW DO YOU BUY AND SELL A STOCK?

You can either go through a stock broker or through an online brokerage account or, more realistically for our age group, through an app. How badass is it to buy, sell, and trade through your frigging phone? It's like being the Wolf of Wall Street at drunk brunch (just kidding, please don't do that).

Essentially you (or an algorithm) determine at what price you want to buy a stock and how many shares you want. That's called a "bid." Those that are selling stocks state how many shares they're willing to sell and at what price. This is called an "offer" or an "ask" price. Technology matches the two people up with the same prices and voila, you have either bought or sold stock.

People usually "buy the dip" or when people are selling. Dips happen for any number of reasons—geopolitical uncertainty, economic conditions, stupid things a leader said—nothing is planned, but you *can* predict highs and lows.

Ideally, you buy what you know and stay away from companies and their stocks that give you a bad feeling. Love Starbucks? Buy SBUX. Hate

This morning has been a roller coaster of emotions and I really hate roller coasters.

"Please don't tell me you pulled the trigger on that trade because it was $69.69."

"It looked... nice?"

Chipotle? Short (sell) or don't buy CMG. You should also buy into trends. For example, our generation will go above and beyond for our pets because we're not monsters and appreciate our fur babies the way they were meant to be treasured. This means investing in high-end pet food brands isn't such a bad idea. Use your common sense, go with your gut on sensible risks, and maybe take a well-earned vacation with the extra cash you earned. Or pay off some of your student loans. Either works.

Now we're going to go over some retirement plans and how to safely and effectively manage your money. This is in the vain hope that our generation can eventually retire and not have to send those "just circling back!" emails for the rest of eternity.

WHAT IS A 401(K) AND HOW CAN IT HELP ME?

A 401(k) is a popular retirement plan that allows employees to set pre-tax dollars aside for that lofty goal of retirement. The money you save is taken out of your income and not taxed until you take it out and use it, ideally during retirement (duh) when you're in a much lower tax bracket than you were while working.

Employer contributions are essentially free money—free money you'd be a fool to not take advantage of because it's one of the perks of full-time employment versus the gig economy.

Employer contributions are usually a percentage of your salary they'll deposit that matches the amount you put in, dollar for dollar, up to a certain amount. You'll want to pay careful attention to 401(k) matching while you're considering a new job and its benefits.

Investing your 401(k)

Now, how to make money with your retirement savings? Some companies may present you with pre-made portfolios you can choose from, others offer a bunch of different mutual funds and allow you to allocate certain percentages of your retirement to the respective funds.

Because you're younger, you can take more financial risks than someone who's about to put their ungrateful kid through college, retiring, or starting their own theme bar/petting zoo.

This means someone in their early 20s should have 20% of their portfolio in more conservative investments like money markets and bonds, and 80% in more lucrative, yet-volatile options like stocks, commodities, and real estate. Should you be paying attention to your 401(k) even though you have the option to set it and forget it? Absolutely.

You'll want to assess risk versus performance. Keep an eye on how much money you're making off your investments and if you're not happy, pull it out and stick it somewhere else. Your money should be working for you, not the other way around.

ROTH IRA

Aside from sounding like the name of a Jewish uncle, a Roth IRA is a retirement account that allows you to add as much as $5,500 a year. The cool thing about a Roth IRA is that whatever you earned over the years plus the withdrawal itself is tax-free if you take it out over age 59-and-a-half. I know that's a lot to put away each year, but you'll be very happy with yourself at age 60. It's not like social security will still be around by then, so anything you can squirrel away is an excellent idea.

WHAT IS A MUTUAL FUND?

A mutual fund is something you'll probably find in your 401(k), but you don't have to have a 401(k) to invest in one. You take a chunk of money and pool it with other investors, and a company like Fidelity, or Vanguard, or a bank invests it for you.

Mutual funds have the advantage of owning stocks, bonds, and cash, so you're better diversified. For example, if the stock market crashes, which it tends to do on occasion, you'll lose money on stocks but your bonds and cash might be okay.

The gist of a mutual fund is: you're giving a smaller amount of money with a bunch of other people and reaping the benefits of someone else's expertise in investing it. You might have to pay some fees, but it's not a bad idea. There are different mutual funds you can invest in that will pay dividends or concentrate on certain sectors, and if you do your homework, you can find mutual funds without the frills or fees.

WHAT'S A CD?

A certificate of deposit, or CD, is a savings account that you can't withdraw from until it "matures" on a certain date. Instead of betting on a fluctuating stock market, the CD has a fixed interest rate so you know exactly how much money you'll make out of it. A normal timespan for a CD can range from three months to five years.

It's a very boring but very safe investment, and the CDs with better rates are usually found online. As of right now, the best rate I can find is 2.8 annual percentage yield (APY) with a $500 minimum deposit.

SHOULD I GET A FINANCIAL ADVISOR?

It's not a bad idea, but they're going to take fees. In a nutshell, most financial advisors use ratios to figure out what percentage of your personal income will go to necessary expenses like housing and utilities and car payments, what age you'll want to retire, and at what point you'll want to buy a home. They then use that information to make investment judgments for you.

Budgeting with a financial advisor is where you'll need to be devastatingly honest with yourself: your wants, your needs, and where you see the future heading. It's a scary proposition but keeping your mighty budget in mind will allow you to conquer any money woes or fears—through ingenuity, grace, or budgeting apps. I sincerely suggest the latter because the two former options are less easy to download.

HOW MUCH AM I ALLOWED TO BLOW ON RENT?

You shouldn't be spending more than 28% of your monthly income on your rent or mortgage. Unfortunately, if you're living in NYC, San Francisco, Seattle, or other cities where rent or mortgages are the stuff of nightmares, then this rule goes out the window. But how much you're blowing on a closet-sized bedroom should be taken into consideration (wistfully stares at my reflection).

HOW MUCH MONEY SHOULD I HAVE IN EMERGENCY SAVINGS/A FUCK OFF FUND?

I cannot stress enough the importance of having a fund available that can get you out of a bad situation, emergency, or job loss. I know this is a lot of liquid cash and it may be impossible when you're first starting out, but you should ideally have 3-6 months worth of cash accessible. Bad things happen occasionally—financially prepare for it if you can.

HOW IS AN EMERGENCY FUND DIFFERENT FROM SAVINGS?

Your savings don't have to be liquid, and are preferably invested in a savings account you aren't touching. You should be putting at least 5-10% of your money in savings for larger ticket items like property, cars, or paying for children—it seems that spawn are always more expensive than you think.

PAY OFF YOUR CREDIT CARDS

A credit card is not a fun coupon. It is connected to your line of credit that is attached to your name, and wild spending may be fun in the moment but could take years to correct. That mental health week where you rented your own private island and filled it with strippers may have been killer Instagram fodder, but it wasn't your best moment financially.

Emergencies like medical bills, repairs to your car or home, and urgent travel are the only huge ticket items you should be putting on your credit card. Otherwise limit your CC spending to what you can actually pay off at the end of the month. Even just covering the minimum will save you from paying off stupid amounts of interest to the bank.

KEEP A CUSHION IN YOUR CHECKING ACCOUNT
A cushion is an extra couple hundred dollars to a grand in your checking account, so if you absentmindedly pay off a lot of bills at once or make a big

debit card purchase, you won't get hit with overdraft fees.

You never want to keep a ton of money in your checking account because that's money not working for you, but having a little extra in there just to be safe will offer you peace of mind, and not make you feel sick when you see your ATM receipts.

But what if I want to go big and go home?

BUYING BIG STUFF, LIKE HOUSES AND CARS

First of all, congrats! This is a huge life step that shouldn't be taken lightly. Pat yourself on the back and realize how this purchase may affect almost every facet of your life. You're going to have to turn to financing or apply for credit to pay for it so you should *really* love it.

A rule of thumb is to not base your big purchases on how you feel in the moment, considering you're going to have to live with this decision for a while.

HOMES

When buying a home, assume you're going to live in it for at least the next five to ten years. Is your life going to change dramatically? Will you still like the neighborhood? Are you planning on getting married, knocked-up, or impregnating someone? These are all considerations you should take into account not, "Oh, interest rates are so low and I'm tired of not being able to make the tastefully erotic gallery wall of my dreams while renting so, YOLO."

Another one of the big questions you have to ask yourself while purchasing a home or condo: can you comfortably afford a 20% down payment?

The cost of your home shouldn't be more than three times the amount of money you make in a year, before taxes. Anything more and your mortgage will probably exceed 28% of your gross income. You also need to factor in other expenses, like property taxes, which are a hell of a lot more than you expect. There could also be condo fees and maintenance fees, which take their toll.

My friend Brian Caggiano, Editorial Manager at Brooks Brothers, has bought both a condo and home, so I wanted to know his thoughts on home costs:

> "Initially, I went back and forth on buying in the suburbs or renting in the city. In the end, it all came down to numbers. Interest rates were still low and I wanted to be able to take advantage. To me, a mortgage payment is easy to swallow because it's a sort of forced saving, especially for me. I imagined moving into the city and squandering the money from my condo sale on bar bills and restaurants etc. Still, I have misgivings because I am subjected to

the commute and there are fewer things to do in the 'burbs. I love the work that comes with a house, I am surprised at how relaxing yard work is, and I love the gratification of completing tasks. The unexpected costs of a home never fail to surprise me though. Often, just to get a repairman out to my house comes with a $100–200 fee before he or she even steps inside."

CARS

Cars can last a while—do you want to be stuck with one, especially in the age of ride-sharing? If you're in an urban area, it might not be worth it. A car comes with additional expenses like insurance, maintenance, parking, gas, tickets, emergencies...you get it.

CREDIT SCORES

Your credit score is like your SAT score, but instead of applying for colleges, you're applying for a loan so you can make one of those aforementioned big purchases.

Credit scores range from 300-850, with 850 being a perfect score. Most people have a score in the 700s. Unless you haven't been paying bills or don't have a credit record (this is why you should really have a credit card), you shouldn't really worry.

Only God and my bartender can judge me.

BUT HOW IS MY CREDIT SCORE CALCULATED?

- **Payment history: 35%**
  This is why you should always pay your credit card bills on time, even if you're only meeting the minimum. Other payments can include student loans, car payments, and your mortgage, if you have one. Rent is not figured in. One of the easiest ways to keep your credit score from sliding is to have automatic payment plans set up so even if you forget, you won't be late.

- **Debt utilization: 30%**
  The less debt you have drawn relative to your total limit, the higher your score will be. Try to keep this as close to 0% as possible, and for sure below 30%

- **Length of credit history: 15%**
  While this may feel wholly unfair and biased against the youth (who are the future, by the way!!), how long you've been paying your bills does factor into your score. To a loan officer reviewing your credit application, little to no credit history is equal to bad history. Sometimes a person with no credit history has a perfect score because of inactivity, but a perfect score arouses suspicion. Kind of like seeing a Tinder bio of a model that attended Harvard who says you should subscribe to their web cam, something's fishy.

How can you get around this? If you were an authorized user on a parent's account, that could work. Or open a credit card as soon as you can and start paying it off to establish some history.

- **Type of credit: 10%**
  Having house or car debt looks a lot better than credit card debt. Student loan debts fall in the middle, which is pretty rude IMO. While there are arguments about good versus bad debt, it's all money that you still owe.

- **New credit: 10%**
  How often your credit is being checked also weirdly affects the score. Neurotically checking your score through your bank's website won't affect it—but if you're applying for a house loan, car loan, and opening new credit cards, the algorithm isn't going to be happy with you. To the algorithm or loan officer, it looks like you're about to take on a ton of debt so why should they lend you money?

WHY THE HELL DOES MY CREDIT SCORE MATTER?

"I am so much more than my credit score," would make a great lower-back tattoo, and a truthful one at that, but credit scores are kind of important if you're applying for a loan, an apartment rental, or mortgage.

Your score lets banks know at a glance if you're dependable, if they should offer credit to you, and if so, how much and under what terms. Your score matters, but it shouldn't be paralyzing. Your bank probably lets you check it for free, but you can also go to US Federal Trade Commission-approved sites to check yours.

 HOW TO SAVE, EVEN WHEN IT FEELS LIKE YOU CAN'T

We've all been in that dark place where you can't feasibly imagine how you can save money in your current financial state. While waiting for the clouds to pass, use every (legal) trick you can to help your sanity and savings account:

HAGGLING! IT STILL EXISTS!
While it may feel extremely awkward to debate a bill, or you just assume some prices are set in stone, they aren't.

- **Renting**
  Your rent, once you sign the lease, is a done deal, but while you're viewing the apartment you can offer a lower price if it's in line with the average rent in your neighborhood. Do your comparative research and come armed with notes if it's not going to be wildly competitive to get the apartment.

  When you're renewing, that's when you really do your research. If and when they raise your rent, use counterpoints and find out what the average rent is in your area. They don't want to lose money on an empty apartment, and you don't want to deal with the emotional and financial hell that is moving.

- **Utilities**
  Other bills with wiggle room include your cell phone and utility bills. Hate your cell plan? Call the company and find one better suited for you, which you may be able to get at a promotional price.

If your electric bill looks wonky—call them! Sometimes the electric company doesn't come to read the meter because of weather or poor planning and delivers an estimated bill. You can put off payment

"Self-care is the greatest luxury," she said to the bartender. "Miss, I can't fill that flower vase up with sangria. It doesn't matter that you 'got a great deal on it.'"

until they send you a more accurate one, or they'll adjust your bills in the coming months to reflect the month you overpaid.

Hospital Bills
For the love of God, fight your hospital bills. Our healthcare system will literally be the death of us all; fight your unfair bills (nicely). Often someone in the hospital's admin office will be able to cut some of the costs, especially if you're younger and have student loans and such.

- **Can't pay a bill? Call the company to set up a payment plan**
This is imperative for larger hospital bills. The good news is, you don't have to pay it off all at once. If you're expecting a large bill, don't sit in the dark, waiting in a cold sweat for the bill to hit your inbox. Call the hospital beforehand, explain your current financial situation, and explore a payment plan. This is also where the haggling comes in. I know it sucks but I promise you will get through this.

No, you cannot choose "muse" as a career path.

BECOMING YOUR OWN COMPANY: SHOULD YOU REGISTER AS AN LLC?

This is a question I had struggled with at length, until I took the plunge at the advice of literally any freelancer that is now living with the new tax code. Do I regret it? Not sure. Check back with me in a few years to see if I'm living in a van down by the river.

THE GIG ECONOMY IS A TRICKY BEAST

"Incorporating" yourself can give you tax breaks and legal protection. If you're a company, then you can write off business expenses as tax deductions. You'll also limit your legal liability—for example if your company goes under or you get sued, your assets can be somewhat shielded. The company is the one taking the hit, not you, even if for all intents and purposes you *are* the company.

WHAT ARE THE TYPES OF ENTITIES?

There are a ton but here are some of the more common ones:

- **Sole proprietorship**
This is when you are the business. It's the simplest, least expensive, and you don't need an accountant while still getting the benefit of deductions. You just don't get the liability protection that comes with other entities.

- **Partnership**
This is when two or more people form the business. There can be multiple partners (hence obnoxiously long names at some law firms)

who can choose how much liability they want. Partnerships allow lower taxes, but offer less liability protection. The reason why people will form partnerships is because the partnership doesn't pay any taxes; it's all dealt with through the partners' tax returns.

- **LLC**

  If you're a small business or a freelancer, this is probably what you'll go with. There are fewer taxes than if you're a corporation, and you get limited liability protection.

- **Corporation**

  Don't make yourself a corporation just because you like the sound of it!! There are two main types of corporations: S corps and C corps.

  An S corporation is limited to 100 shareholders, and you get the liability protection of a corporation, but as a shareholder, all of the expenses and losses are tied to your personal tax return (which is based on your individual share).

  A C corporation is what you think of when someone talks about a Fortune 500 company. There are a lot of taxes involved, but also total liability protection. That's because a corporation is considered a fictitious person by law.

  When it comes to taxes, corporations are taxed at both the state and federal level like they're an individual and then, because you're a shareholder, you're taxed on your personal earnings, too.

WHAT PROTECTION DOES INCORPORATION GIVE?

If the company goes under, only the corporation feels the burn and the shareholders only lose what they invested in the company. Their personal assets are left untouched.

If you're an LLC, you unfortunately don't have this kind of protection. If you get sued, you have to prove that your LLC is legit, and if there isn't enough money in the company, they can go after you! Fun, right?

ALTERNATIVE INVESTMENTS

If you're looking to diversify your portfolio even more, you can look into investments that will not only increase in value over the years, but can be enjoyed in the meantime— either as a collector's item or because you're actively using it or turning the investment itself into a hobby.

WINE AND LIQUOR

No. This isn't for your personal bar cart. Collectors that are all about rare wines and spirits will pay a lot for the bottle they're missing.

No, spending $400 at Sephora is not "investing in yourself."

Back in 2007, the Distilled Spirits Council pioneered the legalization of spirits auctions in NY, and the public's infatuation with high-end and premium whiskeys is helping drive the category for collectors as well.

And according to the same group, from 2010–2016, "High End Premium" and "Super-Premium American Whiskey" were on a tear. High End Premium revenues were up 44 percent and Super-Premium revenues were up 141 percent. In 2017, American whiskey was up 8.1 percent of $252 million to $3.4 billion. Buying a bottle of something you love and storing it appropriately might appreciate in value over time, and worst-case scenario, you drink it. Kind of a win-win situation.

Wine auctions are also the stuff of legends, with bottles going for the cost of some homes. There are a few things to consider before you invest in wine or liquor:

- **Insurance and storage costs**
  These are bottles you can't just stick in a back cabinet; can you afford to insure and house them?

- **Commission costs for auction houses**
  Do you want an auction house taking a chunk of what you end up getting?

- **Do your research**
  There are always wonky regulations that determine what you can buy and where, make sure to do the homework on your state.

  Before all is said and done, you also need to do your research on the bottle's scarcity and its current and future value. This isn't a, "Oh, I like this brand so I'm going to buy a case of it and leave it in the basement for a decade" sort of investment. You need to immerse yourself in it, follow your own personal tastes, and consider what you think will be trending.

JEWELRY

Jewelry, precious stones, and metals can grow in value. They also make fun gifts, especially when they're to yourself. My dad's an estate jeweler, so here's what the illustrious Harold Solomon of Harry H. Solomon Estate Buying Group had to say about buying jewelry (the smart way).

- **Types of jewelry that will gain in value as collectibles**
  Older, signed pieces that aren't in hundreds of stores are always a good buy. Signed, trademarked items that come from popular luxury designers like Tiffany and Cartier also won't lose their value if they're quality pieces. They'll especially gain value as collectibles if the designer has passed away or the collection is no longer available.

Reminder: if he went to Jared or actually thinks a kiss begins with Kay, shut that shit down now.

- **FANCY COLORED DIAMONDS**
  Right now, fancy certified diamonds are doing well, especially pink and blue gems, but keep in mind it's only a passing trend. In the 60s and 70s you couldn't give them away. Another example of certified fancy diamonds not retaining value are yellow diamonds. In the 90s and 00s, they were extremely popular, and now they're still expensive but not as highly valued as they once were.

- **COLORED STONES**
  Surprise—rubies, sapphires, and emeralds are precious stones rather than diamonds. If they're a lab-certified, unheated color you'll get a good price for them. To give you a better idea of the landscape: 99% of colored stones are heated to intensify the color.

  For a fee, Laboratories like American Gem Lab (AGL) or Gübelin will tell you not only if the stone has been heated, oiled, or filled to make it look better, but also where the stone was mined.

In terms of sapphires, unheated Kashmir with exceptional color brings the highest prices. For rubies, it's unheated Burma.

- **MAKE SURE YOUR STONE IS CERTIFIED FROM A GOOD LAB**
  A Diamond Certification is a special document you receive from a third-party lab that reviews the diamond and all its characteristics. The tricky part is that diamond certifications are not created equal, and it needs to come from a reputable grading company.

  The most highly regarded and traded diamond report is from GIA (The Gemological Institute of America). The second best is the AGL report from the AGTA (American Gem Trade Association). The third would be the EGL (European Gem Lab), but only if from the US Lab.

- **PAY ATTENTION TO DIAMOND SHAPES**
  The popularity of other shapes come and go, but round has the best track record. Keep that in mind when buying engagement rings if you are not sold on what shape or design to get.

CRYPTOASSETS

Cryptocurrencies are all the rage right now, and not just for dark-web purchases. The blockchain technology that cryptocurrencies is built on can involve everything from investing to food-safety, but we're going to focus on its currency uses today. I'm definitely not well-versed in the subject, but

I made "explain Bitcoin to me" my Tinder bio and you should see some of the batshit messages I'm getting.

Jeremy Gardener, co-founder and Managing Partner of Ausum Ventures, very much is:

> "The emergence of blockchain technology and cryptoassets is perhaps the most revolutionary human development since the internet. They enable the disintermediation of middlemen across every industry, from payments to healthcare, music to real estate—returning value to producers and consumers. Investing in cryptoassets is a daunting task, with many scams and endless speculation. Just as with the stock market, most investors should stick to the 'blue chips' like Bitcoin and Ethereum, but even with those investments you should not put in more money than you can afford to lose. With more education, one can expand their investments into other, more novel cryptoassets. The appreciation potential of this asset class is unparalleled, but it is just as easy to lose money, so be careful!"

HOUSES

If you fit all of the aforementioned qualifications for being a home-buyer (essentially knowing you want to stay there awhile and able to provide a 20% down payment), then real estate is an awesome investment.

A growing trend is buying your vacation home before your "real" home, if you plan on living in the city a while longer, and can't afford or don't want to buy an apartment there.

Ah, Friday night or, "Pass out in a Restoration Hardware until they threaten you with trespassing."

It's more common for younger couples that aren't ready for kids and don't want to move to the suburbs yet to pull the trigger on this because, DINK (double-income-no-kids) money is a powerful force. You can also rent out that weekend home if it's in a prime area (like a waterfront) for extra cash, which helps justify the investment.

YOURSELF

Yes, you can invest in yourself. Things like education or training tools to further you in your career can all be considered an investment, especially if your salary will jump with it. But no, your self-care skincare routine doesn't count.

Let's hear from an expert. Carleton English, former wealth advisor and current financial journalist, lays down some best practices for those of us that could use a helping hand in the financial literacy department:

No, you cannot go to grad school for self-care.

- **ON SAYING NO**

  "The best financial advice I heard that I wish I could take credit for is: 'Don't let other people spend your money.' What does this mean? Say no to the birthday dinners, destination weddings, bachelorette weekends, and all the other invites that come up in your 20s that you can't fully afford but begrudgingly agree to while becoming increasingly enslaved to your credit card company and its double-digit interest rates. Good friends will understand, bad friends will disappear even before their first marriage dissolves.

- **ON CONSOLIDATING DEBT**

  While we're on the topic of debt, many millennials feel trapped by hefty student loan balances and credit card debt. Unfortunately, there is no easy way out of debt, but that doesn't mean that people should feel completely powerless about their finances.

  Always strive to negotiate better interest rates on any debt you have. Making the first phone call to creditors is intimidating because people don't realize the power they have as consumers of credit. Think of it this way: a credit card company would rather have a good customer pay a lower interest rate than have that customer go to a competitor or, even worse, default on their debt. The worst the company can say is 'no.' And if that's their answer, consider taking your business elsewhere.

  Does a lower interest rate mean that your debt will magically go away? Bahaha, of course not. But it will help immensely when it comes to paying off debt faster.

On that line, there are two competing schools of thought on how to best pay off debt. The first says to pay the highest interest debt most aggressively (typically credit cards) while making minimum payments on other debt.

The second method is called the snowball method, which says to pay off your smallest debts first—perhaps the $150 on a store credit card—while making the minimum payments on the larger debts. Once one debt is paid off, use that money to make payments on other debts and repeat.

The first method will likely save you money in interest payments. The second method appeals to people's psychological feelings of accomplishing something.

Which one is best? The one that gets *you* out of debt fastest. Everyone is different. If the snowball method works for you, do it. Yes, it may mean more in interest payments but if chipping away at a seemingly insurmountable debt load under the first method leaves you loading up on debt elsewhere, it's not really working, is it?

In some cases, it may make sense to consolidate your debt. An accredited credit counseling agency—not the junk mail that arrives in your mailbox—will speak with your creditors to negotiate a lower interest rate and perhaps a lower balance. All of your debt will lumped together so that you're making one monthly payment. Again, your debt does not disappear but it becomes easier to manage with a firm payoff date looming in the future. During this time, however, your ability to get new credit may be constrained.

- **ON DIPPING YOUR TOE INTO INVESTING**
While some millennials struggle with debt, others are ready to grow their fortunes. (You can, theoretically, do both at the same time—pay debt while saving and investing.)

New investors wishing to open a brokerage account will want to look where the trading and management fees are low.

A lot of people seem to think investing automatically means investing directly in stocks—something that tends to terrify Great Recession-scarred millennials. Low-cost index funds are a perfectly reasonable first investment for people who aren't ready to research their favorite stocks. An index fund—such as one that follows the S&P 500—will also provide quick diversification.

Many say you shouldn't invest until you have 3-6 months of living expenses saved in cash. This is perfectly fine advice but not entirely practical for many millennials who feel they'll never hit that mark. A millennial with little to no debt may be able to start investing once they have 1–2 months of expenses saved. They can then gradually build up their cash and investment portfolio from there."

CHAPTER 6

Entertaining

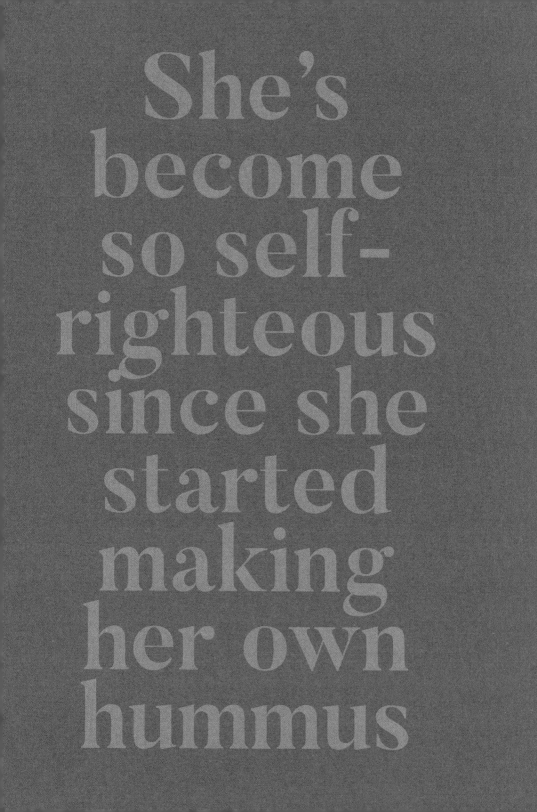

She's become so self-righteous since she started making her own hummus

Having friends over always seems like a good idea. You're in control of your surroundings, not paying exorbitant bar prices, and in the morning you'll most likely wake up to a lot of excess alcohol. Most importantly, you'll be in close proximity to your own bed.

While this is all excellent in theory, you don't want to get in the habit of hosting all the time because it'll get exhausting, expensive, and grating. A slutty friend will always bring their flavor of the week, someone exclusively carts along the terrible liquor you thought you left behind in college, and another always ends the night passed out on your couch. You're not a halfway house for post-grads, (some of whom make way more money than you because nepotism is a tricky beast).

Go with a happy medium and provide an appropriate amount of food and booze, and if a lot of people are coming over relegate grocery items to your closer friends so you don't end up with 15 bottles of wine with nothing to soak it all up.

Hanna Howard, a New York-based lifestyle editor, is no stranger to hosting 30-some people in her Upper East Side studio apartment. Seriously—her holiday parties get more extravagant every year and I've been attending them since our early twenties.

Because my studio can host little more than pitchers of mixed drinks and carb-heavy appetizers before I force everyone to go to a more spacious bar, I asked her for some of her entertaining tips for small spaces:

"Hosting a party when you live in a cramped space—thanks to the high rent in your city, your low-paying job, or a happy mix of the two—can seem overwhelming. Luckily, people in their twenties have low standards. Make even a minimal effort (a cheese plate, a few bottles of wine from Trader Joe's) and you'll suddenly have a reputation as the 'fancy' friend. That said, there are a few things you can do when hosting that'll really make you feel like you've earned that title.

MAKE IT COZY

If you're not having a specifically seated event (like a dinner party), congratulations! You don't have to do too much reorganizing; just make sure your place is clean. But you do have to make sure there's enough seating for at least a fair amount of the people who come by, even if it's technically standing room only.

Turn your bed into a seating area by covering it with a blanket; cover the pillows too, you don't want to worry about them when you're sliding under the covers after your guests leave. If you have stools or small chairs, put them in different places to create seating areas that aren't just around the coffee table or couch. This will allow your guests to have smaller seated groups—perfect if you're inviting a few different friend groups who don't like to mingle.

DON'T OVERDO IT

Think about what's reasonable in your space. Most people are just happy a friend is hosting anything at all—especially if your social life usually consists of standing in crowded bars with overpriced drinks—so if the best you can do is order in or put together a cheese board and other store-bought snacks, that's perfectly OK. Consider what's reasonable for you to do in the prep time you have and given your skill set. If you know your three-course dinner with wine pairings will go off without a hitch because of your impeccable timing and cooking, go for it. But don't feel like anything less is a failure.

BE SPECIFIC

Encouraging your friends to bring some or all of the booze for the evening is a good way to make people feel like they're contributing with a very easy lift. If you're making something specific though, and need a certain amount of particular drinks, be absolutely clear when people ask what they can bring. That way you don't end up with a 12-pack of PBR when what you really needed were a couple bottles of prosecco.

BE REALISTIC

We'd all love to throw lavish parties where we can invite our friends, our coworkers, all their plus-ones, and those eight guys on Tinder you've been talking to but haven't actually met. But if you're living in a 400-square-foot studio, you have to cap the guest list somewhere. When I throw a party I start with the list of my absolute invites (my closest friends) and work from there. All of their names go on the list, and anyone with a serious significant other— i.e. not just some guy they're dating—gets a plus one. Depending on the size of the party, I then work my way out to coworkers, and friends of friends, and plus-ones of those people until I hit my personal invite cap."

If you have the space, like my friend and entertainer-extraordinaire Dean Zacharias, then he suggests a more balls-to-the-wall party planning approach:

"Spend half the time on the menu and double on the guest list. Boring guests will destroy an evening (regardless of how great your tablescape may be). A guest list should be wild...filled with your most passionate, interesting acquaintances regardless of political affiliation, age, career, job title, or any other insignificant categorical reference point.

My favorite way to end an evening of entertaining is to be surrounded by the last remaining five or six guests at 2:00 a.m. who are all so different you question how the hell you're in the same room together. This is the sign of a job well done."

A drinking game but for when anyone asks you why you're not going to grad school.

BAR CART ESSENTIALS

Entertaining at our age, unless you're extra fabulous and competent, is going to mostly center around booze. This is why it's not the worst idea to keep a well-stocked bar cart in case of impromptu hosting or an existential crisis. If you're keeping your liquors and mixers in a curated spot, then you also have the benefit of it looking like you've got your shit together (at least aesthetically), rather than a cry for help.

Bar carts go all the way back to the Victorian era when they were actually tea carts, which were rolled in when you wanted to throw a banger. They really had their moment in the sun in the 1950s, when hostessing became an art and cocktail hour was a daily occurrence. (As was smoking and drinking while pregnant, so you can decide for yourself how healthy the behavior of the *Leave It to Beaver* crowd was.)

Now, thanks to anyone with internet access believing they're an interior designer, bar carts are once again a unisex staple. Every low-end to upscale home goods store carries them, and whichever cart you choose should complement the existing aesthetics of your apartment while staying within your price range.

If you don't feel like blowing dough on a bar cart (and they can get pricey), just convert an existing piece of furniture. Bookshelves, side tables, and nightstands, or even large trays (butler trays) placed on a solid surface can easily be bastardized into a makeshift bar. As long as it comfortably holds booze, various accouterments, and is easily accessible, you're golden.

Now, what the hell to add to it? In a perfect world, your bar cart would hold:

- Tools: jigger, shaker, strainer, bottle opener, corkscrew, whiskey stones, ice bucket, tongs
- Basic boozes: vodka, gin, rum, tequila, whiskey, vermouth.
- Mixers: tonic water, bitters, juice, soda.
- Serveware: highball and old-fashioned glasses, wine glasses, decanter, wine bucket.
- Additions: cocktail onions, olives, etc.

However, because it's your bar cart, you can put whatever the hell you want on it. To truly make it your own, add personalized accents that give it character, like playing cards, swizzle sticks, matchbooks, and anything you've drunkenly stolen from a higher end bar (just kidding, please don't do that).

BATCHING

When you're making large quantities of drinks for your thirsty guests, there's unfortunately going to be some math involved. Luckily, it's pretty simple and boils down to:

Your chosen cocktail recipe measurements *x* number of servings you want to make = your batch measurements

Wish I could travel back in time and reassure my younger, more naive self that I'll never have to use calculus again.

I enjoy making this easy rum party drink recipe in batches because A) it's easy to multiply by the number of guests, B) who doesn't enjoy rum year round, and C) it's just sweet enough without resulting in a terrible hangover the next morning.

Can you please stop referring to my glassware as "unimpressively phallic"?

Single Drink Recipe

1oz Lime Juice

.75oz Simple Syrup

2oz Flor de Caña 4-year Rum

Mix well in a shaker with ice

DECANTERS ARE YOUR FRIENDS

So you'll drink rubbing alcohol if necessary—good for you! That kind of go-getter attitude is what will get you through life; the ability to take lemons and add shitty vodka for a questionably good time.

If you don't want your friends seeing what sad brands of booze you're enjoying, then pour them into decanters. Sometime it's best not to know, and (nice) decanters create a really great aspirational lie.

THE MYTH, THE LEGEND, THE CHEESE PLATE

Cheese plates may photograph well but can quickly escalate in price when you opt for several cheeses, meats, nuts, and spreads. Just because it looks great on Pinterest doesn't mean you want to blow $50+ on an elaborate platter that will be drunkenly consumed in ten minutes by a wolf-pack of finance analysts who haven't slept all week.

If you're trying to keep it on the lower end, stick with a hard cheese (like Manchego), soft cheese (like Camembert or Brie), a jam, crackers, and lupini beans.

"I'm attainable luxury," she explained to her wheel of Costco brie. It remained silent.

My friend Brian turned me on to lupini beans and they're a great, cheap, and easy option your guests will love. Simply drain the jar, toss the beans in olive oil and a little salt, and they're good to go. You can even eat the shells (because instant gratification should be one the main tenets of eating), but leave an extra bowl out for shell disposal nonetheless.

If you're really committed to the *proper* cheese board, or will catch hell from your parents if you don't know how to assemble one, here's some of the suggested additions you can choose to include or not. It's your life, and it's certainly your cheese plate.

- Aged: Cheddar, Comté, goat Gouda
- Soft: Camembert, Brie
- Firm: Manchego, Parmigiano-Reggiano, Cheddar, Gouda, Gruyère
- Blue: Gorgonzola dolce, Stilton
- Selection of breads: sliced baguette, bread sticks, crackers (bonus points for water crackers)
- Condiments: jams, honeys, spicy mustard
- Vegetables: artichoke hearts, roasted red peppers, olives, cornichons
- Cured meats: prosciutto, salami, soppressata, chorizo, pâté
- Candied or toasted nuts, dried figs, and fresh grapes all make good additions as well.

Other tips:

- Set the cheese out an hour before serving
- Cut hard cheeses ahead of time
- Label your cheeses so people aren't asking you all night
- Include a respective cheese knife for each cheese

EASYISH APPETIZERS

Hosting is an art form. And, like most artists, you're probably broke.

Now that you have the more important part taken care of (booze), why not figure out what food you're going to

"He died as he lived, unconsciously consuming entire sticks of butter through those viral Facebook recipes."

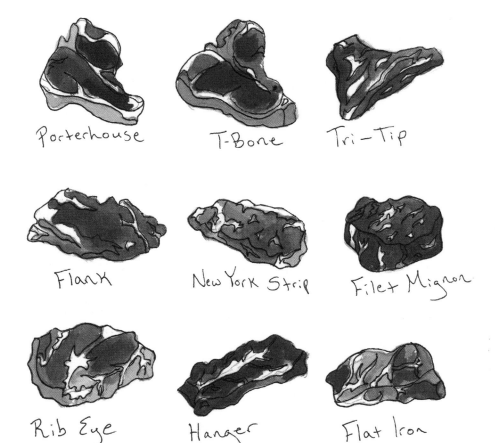

Get to know your cuts of meat.

serve your ravenous guests? Make sure at least one or two of the appetizers served are carb-heavy so it can be force-fed to a lightweight guest that desperately needs sustenance after repeatedly calling an ex after two glasses of wine.

A few things to consider

Know your audience. You're probably (hopefully) friendly with the majority of people who plan on showing up at your place and should be aware if someone has major allergies, doesn't drink, is gluten-free, Kosher, etc.

If you're not positive you can ask in the email invite, or just go full-steam ahead. Those that have dietary restrictions will inherently proceed with caution, and can be encouraged to bring something they can eat or drink.

Other things to consider: what serveware do you have to present your appetizers? This is where your chip-and-dip bowls, trays, and excess cheese boards you drunkenly purchased in your darker hours come in handy. Don't be afraid to bastardize your serveware too if you don't have enough of it; I use my cake stands to serve all manner of hors d'oeuvres when I have people over.

If you don't feel like cooking for the hungry masses, the frozen foods section at any local grocery store should have ample party options you can just heat up in the oven. This is also where warehouse memberships come in handy—I usually head to Costco before I have a party to save on bulk items like cheese, meat, chips, beer, and any dips I don't have the emotional bandwidth to make.

POST-PARTY

Congrats, you threw a successful banger and are currently picking up empty bottles and a random acquaintance who *wayyyyy* overstayed their welcome off your living room floor. What to do with all that excess beer, wine, liquor, and food? The latter is obvious: refrigerate or freeze whatever can be salvaged while tossing anything that met an untimely end (farewell cheese that was left out on the counter, you deserved better).

No, *you're* easy like Sunday morning.

Save unopened liquor, wine, and beer, either for your own purposes or to give as housewarming or host gifts. Toss opened beers, and you can salvage opened wine bottles that are at least half-full. White wine will last for about four days, and red a week. Cap them off as snugly as you can, and store in the fridge. If it's less than half-full, cap them off and save for cooking purposes. Or drink right then and there to solve the dilemma.

If you have open liquors, you can also save them, cook with them, or experiment with infusions, which I wholeheartedly endorse and enjoy. You literally just cut up pieces of whatever you're infusing your liquor with, throw it in a jar with the liquor, and store in a cool dark place for at least a few hours.

My infusing go-tos usually include ginger or jalapeño in vodka, or jalapeño in tequila or mezcal. Liquor infusions also make for great holiday presents when you wrap up smaller batches in a cute jar.

MAKING YOUR SPACE FRIENDLY FOR GUESTS

In terms of acquiring flatware and dinnerware, remember that you're in the very early stages of curating household goods. Unless you're in a more permanent spot, don't beat yourself up over waiting to purchase decent or full sets of dinnerware until you're living sans roommates who won't knock over your crystal. Widely available items from IKEA, Pottery Barn,

Which circle of Hell is the "shabby chic" one?

or Williams-Sonoma's Open Kitchen collection (the lower end of the brand) will do just fine.

If you're in the mood for more off-the-beaten-path kitchenware, then check out flea markets, estate sales, eBay, Etsy, and the like. You can snag entire high-quality settings for a fraction of the price without setting foot into the relationship-ruining labyrinth that is IKEA. Hell, I use a Wedgewood set I found at my local thrift store that was the same price as takeout.

Noted small-space decorator (his post-college, 300-square-foot Chicago apartment was so lovely, it was even featured on Curbed) McKenzie Mullins notes:

> "If you buy and keep only what you love, you'll find you're surrounded by things you love and that is pretty cool. The early 20s are the best and worst years of your life and, like any great drama, the right setting always complements the plot."

I hate myself for mentioning this anecdote but here we go: I was at a friend's apartment and he was complaining about a kitchen appliance. Considering he was a hedge-fund bro, I suggested he and his live-in girlfriend upgrade the appliance, and he noted they wouldn't because they could just register for one when they got around to getting married. Boom. Don't go crazy with the home goods or kitchen gear if you're planning on getting married in the next few years.

HOW TO NOT LOOK LIKE AN IDIOT WHILE YOU'RE OUT IN A FANCY SETTING

Show me an open bar networking event and I'll write you a tragedy.

Whether it's for work or a social setting, unless you grew up with your parents frequently taking you out to nice restaurants, you might not be used to the etiquette and nuances that come with more elevated dining.

There's more on this in the "Etiquette" chapter, but, so you can easily navigate your way around champagne and oysters and the difference among glassware, below are the basics. The important thing is to not feel intimidated by your surroundings and just enjoy the moment (preferably on the company tab).

CHAMPAGNE ETIQUETTE
• Unless you're planning on drinking the champagne within a week, don't keep it in

the fridge. The cork will shrink. Instead, store it on its side in a cool, dark place that's about 50-55°.

- If friends are on their way and you need to chill your champagne quickly, place the bottle in a bucket of half-water and half-ice. Spinning the bottle in the bucket also makes it colder quicker. An ex used to wrap wet paper towels around wine and champagne bottles and stick them in the freezer if we needed them colder quickly (God forbid he had to deal with me sober), but, as a caveat, we weren't drinking expensive bottles.

- To open a champagne bottle properly, hold it at a 45° angle while keeping your thumb on the cork (never pointing the bottle at anyone, that's very important) and turn the cage six times. Stretch the cage out with your thumb still on the cork, and when the cork releases it shouldn't make a popping noise. Wipe the rim of the bottle with a napkin to make sure there's no foil on it, and serve.

- For serving champagne you want champagne glasses, tulip-shaped flutes, or white wine glasses. What you smell is what you taste, so you don't want a wide glass that you would use for red wine.

- Swirl and smell champagne before you sip, like you do with wine. Drink from the same spot on the glass so your lips don't smudge the entire rim.

- When toasting, do not clink glasses, simply make eye contact, sip, and then make eye contact again. Clinking glasses can chip them and your host will not be happy with you if you destroy Great Grandma's champagne coupes.

OYSTER ETIQUETTE

- An oyster fork has three prongs and is located to the right of your plate. It's only used to see if the oyster is "free and clear," meaning it's no longer attached to the shell. You don't eat with it.

- To consume, gently scrape the bottom of your oyster with the fork, place the shell's hinge toward the back of your hand, and place the condiments on it. Then tilt the shell back and gulp it down, or slurp it up if there's visible sediment.

- East Coast oysters are meatier, more savory, and brinier with a saltwater flavor—lemon is usually a good pairing. West Coast oysters are more buttery and good with sweet pairings, like a champagne mignonette.

- Turn the oyster shell over after you've consumed it.

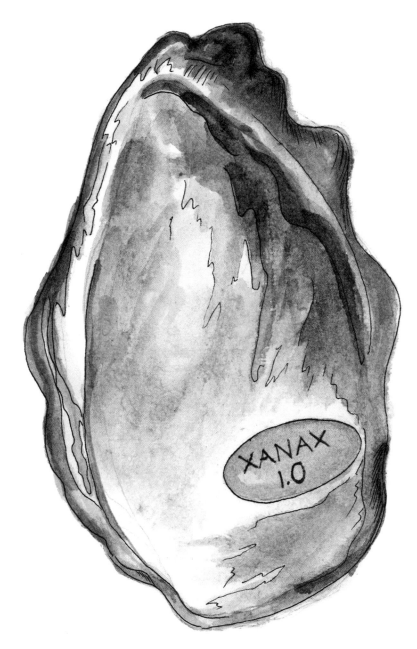

A more useful pearl.

RED WINE

WHITE WINE

COLLINS

COCKTAIL

SNIFTER   HIGHBALL   FLUTE   COUPE   ROCKS

GLASSWARE

Ever wondered why your older friends and mentors have such an extensive glassware collection? It's because each glass is used for different beverages. So you don't get caught off-guard in more elevated drinking or dining situations, here's what to expect with each glassware silhouette.

SHORT TUMBLER

Old fashioneds, whiskey on the rocks, or any manner of non-alcoholic beverages you deem appropriate.

TALL TUMBLER

Used for highballs, more tropical drinks with fruit, iced teas, soda, and any drink that requires a bunch of ice cubes.

WHITE WINE GLASS

A white wine glass has a smaller bowl so there's less space to aerate, and the wine doesn't oxidize too quickly. It also features a longer stem so your body heat won't taint or tarnish the wine's flavor.

Any glass is a wine glass if you *believe* hard enough.

RED WINE GLASS
The bowl is larger on a red wine glass so you can swirl the wine more easily to help aerate it.

COCKTAIL GLASS
This is for martinis, Manhattans, and anything a trite character from *Sex and the City* would be found drinking.

CHAMPAGNE FLUTE
A tall, narrow bowl is placed on a stem for you guessed it—champagne. A smaller surface area helps preserve the bubbles and prevent it from going flat quickly. It can also hold sparkling wines, and champagne cocktails like mimosas.

LIQUEUR GLASS
They look like petite fancy glasses. They're meant for drinking liqueurs and cordials.

BRANDY SNIFTER
A wide bottomed bowl with a short base, it's a drink you cradle in your hand while swirling it to release its bouquet and also look insufferable.

CHAPTER 7

Weddings

I'm glad someone found your **self-destructive** tendencies charming.

The circle of life parades on and your friends are putting rings on each other and you find yourself flying to different coasts every other weekend to celebrate the blessings of love and a themed open bar.

But how do you find a happy medium between time-honored traditions and updated etiquette surrounding weddings with all the hashtags and truly, awkwardly painful engagement photo shoots? The important thing is the promise being made between two people and having their family and friends there to share in the happiness. It's the other, less important details that leave you questioning what to do, wear, and how much to spend.

Most of the time you should just go with your gut—or stick to the following guidelines if you usually make terrible decisions.

It wasn't even noon and an ex had already posted his engagement announcement.

All of the frogs you had to Kiss before meeting your prince(ss) are checking your wedding hashtag.

ENGAGEMENT ANNOUNCEMENTS

THEIRS

The unthinkable has happened and even your sluttiest friends are posting proclamations of spending forever with their best friend across all social platforms. Why they needed a flash mob there to do it is questionable, but you'll forgive this painfully transparent attempt to go viral this *one* time.

Bear in mind that the issue with social media is the ease of sharing, and that includes intimate moments that acquaintances and strangers normally wouldn't be privy to. Congratulate those you care about, and don't pay too much attention to the nagging social anxiety that comes with five people in your Facebook feed simultaneously announcing their engagement. Not everyone is getting engaged but you, even if it sometimes feels that way.

YOURS ◈

First of all, congratulations! You've managed to land someone who wants to see only you naked IRL for the tentative future/forever.

Secondly, it's probably best to wait a day or two before announcing your bliss on social media. You need time to get your head straight and tell family

Instead of "a watched pot never boils" it's "throwing your phone won't make him answer texts in a timely fashion."

and close friends the good news before uploading private, exciting information for people you vaguely remember sucking face with in college. Remember to keep it tasteful, and you're not obligated to listen to wedding planning advice yet if you don't want to. This is your wedding, no matter how much a family member thinks they know best.

BROKEN ENGAGEMENTS

THEIRS

In the case of a called-off wedding, protect your friend's feelings and be thoughtful and conscious of their requisite mourning time. The death of a relationship blows, as does blowing off everyone's expectations of their announced nuptials. Get 'em drunk and remind them that all is not lost. Now they can sleep with other people!!!

If you're trying to make a move on the previously engaged, wait a few weeks before making your intentions obvious, otherwise it looks desperate. Just offer your upbeat words when warranted. If they come to you though, all bets are off. They're clearly not mourning that hard.

YOURS

Life happens and security deposits are lost to function halls and you sleep with your former paramour's bridal party and you move on.

As much as it sucks, you need to let people know as soon as possible that the wedding is off so they can cancel flights and hotel rooms. Post a brief message across social media (if it's easier) and ask your family and friends to help get the word out. You may feel embarrassed or pissed off about this, but this too shall pass.

The important thing is how many years of your life you've taken back for yourself, including the time that would have been allocated to lawyers and the division of assets. Keep your head held high, you dissolved something before it could *really* hurt you.

If it wasn't a mutual decision to call it off, just keep in mind that this would have inevitably happened and use the money that would have been lost in divorce court on yourself. Money isn't everything, but it can be a small boat where large wedding costs are concerned. And your boat isn't going to leave you.

Do you think any #brands will want to sponsor my *Eyes Wide Shut* themed bridal shower?

DO I NEED TO BUY AN ENGAGEMENT OR BRIDAL SHOWER GIFT?

You don't need to buy an engagement party present, but it's always a nice gesture. If it's a more casual affair, then flowers, or wine or booze to help round out the bar should work.

Bridal shower gifts are a must, and you should spend $25-$75 on a gift from the registry. If you want to just get them a larger gift that's coming around the time of the nuptials, then let them know in a card you bring to the shower. Otherwise just factor the cost of the bridal shower gift into how much you're spending overall on the wedding.

WEDDING GIFTS

Giving a wedding gift when you're already paying X amount to travel and stay at a hotel could sting a bit. (Especially when it seems like you're going to a wedding every other weekend.)

Now, how much do you spend on the happy couple? It ranges, depending on how well you know them plus your current financial situation. Don't go broke over some drinking buddies you haven't seen in half a decade—if you and your strained budget don't want to go, politely decline.

Another general rule of thumb is to gift however much it probably cost the couple to have you. If you brought a plus one, the number you give them goes up and/or doubles. Paying less plus the chance of meeting someone at the wedding are two good reasons to *not* bring someone if you're single.

If you're attending the wedding as a plus one, you shouldn't have to bring anything unless you're good friends with the couple as well. The invited person should also accommodate for a hotel, unless you feel like splitting the bill with them. In short, being a plus one *rules*.

In case you're still questioning how South Tampa counts as a destination wedding and how much to give the couple, use this handy sliding scale based on degrees of familiarity.

ACQUAINTANCE $50-$100
Drinking buddy, friend of a friend, or kid of someone your parents play golf with—regardless of your vague connection to the couple, there will be a meal and open bar involved.

Was the line, "Show me a hero & I'll write you a tragedy," about Fitzgerald looking at his checking account?

Whether or not you are confused as to how you made the guest list should help determine if you'll actually go. But if you do, blow $50-$100 per person attending.

COWORKER $50-$100
The 40+ hours a week you see them wasn't enough, and you had to trek out to watch them legally bind themselves to someone they met in a fraternity basement. It might be worth going just to see if their romantic second date of purchasing Plan B in the morning is mentioned in the toasts, but judging by the sheer number of people named Tripp and Muffy that will be in attendance you sincerely doubt it. Toss 'em $50-$100 and double it if you're dragging along a plus one.

DISTANT RELATIVE $50-$100
Distant enough cousins to find them attractive, but close enough you wouldn't do anything about it—if you find yourself attending their wedding, first of all ask yourself, why are you there? Secondly, give them the same amount you would an acquaintance or coworker. Just be sure you're not stingy or your family will talk about it *for years*. Hell, it'll probably be brought up at your funeral.

CLOSE FRIEND $150-$200
Barring a *My Best Friend's Wedding* experience, or your friend's betrothed being a real asshat, you're usually excited to see them get hitched. You should let the present reflect your excitement for the event, and get 'em something decent in the $150-$200 range. But also consider your bridal party, travel, and emotional expenses. At the end of the day, your friend is going to know if you had to deal with more pressing expenditures than getting them a Vitamix off their registry.

CLOSE RELATIVE $150-$200
Whether you like them or not, they're your family and you're stuck with them. And now the person entering the family is also stuck with you and yours. This is where you're required to spend more because depending on how close you are with your family, this is probably a big fucking deal. You're going to have to see them at every major holiday, don't let your gifting them puke-green Pottery Barn towels with the wrong monogram tear you guys apart like a Christmas ham after several martinis.

PURCHASING OFF THE REGISTRY

In most cases it's in your best interest to just get them something off the registry or donate to their honeymoon fund. They already picked out what they wanted, make both of your lives easier and just give it to them. The main takeaway here is to just order something with your credit card that will be delivered with a click of a button rather than dragging your gift to the reception. Not many other people will bring theirs and you'll be the random who brought a blender that their family has to schlep back to their place.

If you want to go off the registry and know their taste well, then all the power to you. I usually give the couple a heads up beforehand that I'm getting them something else instead (and make sure the gift receipt is definitely in there).

WEDDING ATTENDANCE

THEIRS

If you receive a wedding invitation that you definitely want to go to, RSVP as soon as you possibly can. It makes you one less person unaccounted for that they have to chase down, and they'll sincerely appreciate it. It's also not a bad idea to set up price alerts for flights and book the hotel way ahead of time—better safe than sorry, especially when commitments are involved.

The most insufferable people aren't the ones who say they're high maintenance, but the ones who *think* they're low maintenance.

It's imperative to remember that if you're not that close to the couple and don't want to go, *don't go*. No one is holding a gun to your head, just make up a decent excuse as to why you won't be attending and no, "It'll only last six months," isn't a great answer.

Weddings are a financial burden for everyone involved and that can be forgotten in the excitement of the moment. You can't feasibly be traveling across the country for a wedding every weekend unless you can afford it. Don't blow your savings on a bunch of emotional open bars and dancing with sparklers. Send a tasteful gift and your apologies as soon as you can and be done with it.

I'm feeling destructive; I'm wearing all dry clean only.

YOURS

- **If you can't invite them to the wedding**
  If someone is peeved they're not invited to the wedding, first of all fuck them, and secondly just say it was solely budgetary and leave it at that. No one can argue with your wedding budget and to do so is cruel and unusually weird. Money is a very personal thing and they're not marrying you or paying for the wedding, so who are they to judge your guest list?

- **If they're not attending your wedding**
  Say something at the right place and time when warranted if you're pissed that they can't make the wedding, but leave it at that. You already have enough on your plate, don't let one or several absences spoil your big day. They might have a legitimate timing conflict or don't have the cash to blow on what may be a fiscally impossible weekend for them. Plus, now you don't have to pay for them and can open up those empty spots to family members or friends that didn't make the first cut.

Did they really have to make the hashtag #AboutDamnTime?

SOCIAL MEDIA AT WEDDINGS

Social media has become a huge part of wedding celebrations, with hashtags curating everything from engagements, bridal showers, and bachelor parties to the nuptials themselves. Even the honeymoons aren't safe from the hashtags' all-encompassing reach. Good luck trying to burn that Instagram of rose petals littering the bed from your mind!

Social media rules for other people's big day include putting your phone away if the couple or officiant asks, not sharing photos of the bride before she walks down the aisle (DUH), and not sharing unflattering photos for which the bride or groom will want to kill you.

The other issue with taking photos and sharing them during the ceremony or reception is you don't want to spend the whole wedding on your phone. In theory you're there to see people you care about get hitched, live in the moment or whatever.

With that said, if there's a wedding hashtag, it's implied that the couple wants and expects you to post to social media.

Are there "thank you for not making me a bridesmaid" cards?

WEDDING ETIQUETTE

Weddings are great because most of the time your only obligation is to show up and celebrate love. However that means unless it's your big day, you have to play by the rules. The couple was gracious enough to invite you, return the good feelings with decorum and respect and not getting so blackout drunk you hit on the groom's mom.

- If you're female—never, ever wear white to a wedding unless it's specifically stated on the invitation. Black is the safest color.

- Men can wear a white dinner jacket if it's a formal summer wedding.

- Don't offer the bride and groom a ton of planning advice (unless asked). Weddings are very personal and you don't want to throw even more options at them or make them second guess their choices; there's already enough stress involved.

- If you're a bridesmaid, you're there for emotional support, not manual labor. If the bride thinks so, it may be time to get a new friend. However, the maid of honor is tasked with throwing the bridal shower and anything the bride requests before the big day arrives. At this point I'd like to thank my mother for only giving me a male sibling.

- If someone has been dating their significant other for less than a year, they don't require an invitation. On that note, a single person doesn't have to be offered a plus one.

- If you need to narrow down the guest list, crossing off people that didn't know the bride and groom as a couple is a good start.

- Don't assume your children are welcome. No one wants kids at an open bar reception. If you really want to bring them, check with the bride and groom first.

- You don't have to invite someone to your wedding just because they invited you to theirs. Everyone has different budgets and venue sizes, you're not obligated to anyone.

- If you know someone can't make it to the wedding but you care about them (less mobile older relatives, for instance) send them an invitation so they still feel included.

- You may have heard that you have up to a year after the wedding to send a gift to the couple. Nope, it's three months. Any more time and they'll probably think you forgot.

- Don't bring your gift to the wedding—the safest thing is to buy something off the registry and then the store can place it on hold for them until the couples decides when they want it to be delivered. There will most likely be a table for gifts and cards, but there's a chance for card theft, even at the most lovely venues.

- This goes without saying, but don't Venmo the bride and groom as their wedding present. Unless they want the cold, hard cash and asked for Venmo in lieu of a check.

Did anyone having a Gatsby themed wedding read the book?

DIVORCE

THEIRS

Shit happens and *forever* isn't always a viable option. When a split happens it's probably for the best anyway, but the division of friends can be a precarious one. If you were originally the friend of one party you'll probably end up staying on their side on the emotional divide, but you're more than allowed to stay friends with both. If one half of the former couple cries foul about your staying in touch with the other, they've made your decision for you.

Divorce is *not* a social taboo and you should stay on your friend's case about getting out there when they're emotionally ready. Don't let them wallow in their own sadness for too long—how else are they going to find some new stranger?

YOURS

First of all, this isn't the end of the world. It's a painful new beginning, but a beginning nonetheless. You had an identity before you met your former partner, and that identity still remains and deserves so much more.

On the bright side, you're somewhat free to go off the rails a bit! This is a major life event, so if you need to take some time to travel and find yourself again, go right ahead (within reason). If you don't have kids, you have a somewhat easier division of assets and no shame in making yourself the priority for a bit. At the end of the day *everyone's* most important relationship is the one with themselves. Treat yo'self because you're the only you you've got.

PARENTS' DIVORCE

This is going to be a hard one to swallow regardless of your age or how much you depend on your parents. Accepting that your parents are also flawed people who deserve a relationship better suited to their current needs sucks. This doesn't discredit your childhood memories or what you perceived as a healthy (or unhealthy) relationship, it just is what it is.

There is no etiquette surrounding this because you have to go with your own gut. Be at least civil to their new significant others if or when they appear, and deal with any infidelity that caused it however you feel best. Forgiveness can be earned, or at least supplemented with time. Hell, sometimes even bought (only half-joking).

"Not sure the family will appreciate your *Valley of the Dolls* themed menu."

"They will when they see the calorie count."

SECOND, THIRD, AND FOURTH WEDDINGS

After a few years of bliss or feigned happiness for the sake of children/parents/social media, it's time for your friends to move on to the next life partner or younger sex toy.

Which number wedding it is shouldn't discount their happiness, but if they've already had one (or several) you really don't need to give as large a gift as you did at their first wedding. The size and cost of the reception should require less fanfare, gauge the present by how good of friends or family they are and proceed accordingly.

WHAT IF YOU DON'T LIKE THE PERSON YOUR FRIEND IS MARRYING?

One of the hardest parts of growing up is seeing your friends marry people that you think are somewhat undeserving of your friend's love and amazing qualities, but that's your cross to bear, not your friend's.

You should have told them that little tidbit while they were still dating, preferably in the earlier stages when they had a lot less to lose by letting the relationship go. That being said, speak up if you have proprietary information such as that their fiancé(e) is actively cheating on them, but otherwise keep your mouth shut. Your friend is very likely going to choose their spouse-to-be over you, and will not be thrilled with your negative opinion.

TBH you'll probably lose them as a friend or be uninvited to the wedding, so choose your battles wisely.

Live your best life—in denial.

WEDDING DRESS CODES, DECIPHERED

Literally put your best foot forward by knowing what the specified dress codes mean before you show up overdressed to a casual backyard service or underdressed to your college roommate's second wedding. Who really shouldn't be throwing *another* black tie function in her early twenties, but it's silly to waste a perfectly good country club membership, isn't it?

When all else fails and you're still unsure, take photos beforehand and share with friends who aren't afraid to tell you the cold, hard truth about poor tailoring and shoe choices.

WHITE TIE

The fanciest of them all! You'll rarely have to deal with this. It's relegated to the Met Galas and White House Dinner-level parties most of us are rudely not invited to.

Women should wear a floor-length evening gown and men should wear a long, black jacket with tails, a formal white shirt, white vest and bow tie, white or gray gloves, and formal black shoes.

BLACK TIE

The second most formal but with some wiggle room. Ladies should go for a floor length dress or something more ornate and paired with extravagant accessories if you choose a midi- or cocktail-length option.

Gentlemen—make it easier on yourselves and opt for a tuxedo. If you don't foresee yourself dramatically losing or gaining weight in the near to distant future and it's in your budget, buy a tux and get it tailored instead of renting. The number of times you'll end up wearing it will be more economical and so much less of a hassle than renting. Also drag out your black bow tie, vest or cummerbund, and patent leather dress shoes.

If it's the summer and you want to go full James Bond, shoot for a white dinner jacket and black tuxedo pants.

CREATIVE BLACK TIE

Ah the auspicious "fun" black tie, which allows you to inject more personality or the designated theme of the night into your attire. Take your cues from black tie requirements, but ladies can wear something a bit more fashion forward and gentlemen can opt for patterned ties or colored vests or cummerbunds.

For example, if it's a luau themed creative black tie, ladies can go with an upscale tropical dress and gentlemen can ditch the black tie and leather shoes for brightly printed neckwear and smoking slippers.

In short, keep it elevated but with enough flair so the theme or your "creative" sartorial choices are subtly to glaringly apparent.

BLACK TIE OPTIONAL

Essentially dudes can choose between a tux or suit and ladies should go with a black tie dress because the patriarchy is very much alive and well. Also, why wouldn't you go full black tie whenever you have the option? Life is too short not to wear your black tie attire whenever humanly possible.

COCKTAIL

Ladies—wear a cocktail dress. Ta-da! Gentlemen, throw on your suit. Because it's cocktail attire you can be less stodgy than you would be for a formal occasion and have fun with your tie, socks, and pocket square.

FESTIVE ATTIRE

Go with your gut depending on the event and time of day for this one. Have fun with your look and spice it up with sequins, bolder colors, and patterns... whatever floats your boat.

If it's daytime, opt for more playful patterns and colors and amp it up with

> **"I know it was a nautical theme but their only referring to each other as co-captains throughout the ceremony and the entire waitstaff dressed in sailors' uniforms was a bit much."**

some accessories. For example, ladies can throw on a cocktail dress and an array of bangles and other eye-catching extras. At night, the sequins and embellishments come out in full force.

Gentlemen can put on a suit of their choice but have more fun with the shirt, tie, pocket square, or sock choices.

GARDEN PARTY OR BEACH FORMAL

One of the more fun summer dress codes, this allows you free reign while taking the environment you'll be gracing your presence with into account.

A garden party will—wait for it—take place in the garden, so ladies can go with a floral or appropriately summery dress. Or go full Slim Aarons with a caftan. Opt for wedges or flats so you don't sink into the grass or are teetering on cobblestone walkways all night.

Gentlemen can go for light-colored, linen suits or a more vibrant blazer and pants situation. Full-on preppy nightmares are encouraged at this kind of event. If you're not feeling that vibe, go with a navy blazer, white shirt, chinos and loafers.

Beach formal is exactly that—it's formal, but remember, you're on a beach. There's sand and waves and seaweed and seagulls that could attack you if you feed them your bread basket after an hour or two of the open bar.

Ladies can play with a more windswept or nautical look, and remember the whole sand bit when you're choosing shoes; heels will not be your friends. Open toed sandals will suffice.

Gentlemen can take the same cues from the garden party look, but with a more seafaring theme instead of a landlocked one.

SEMI-FORMAL OR DRESSY CASUAL

Slightly less formal than cocktail, but not quite casual attire. Think of it as what you'd wear out to a nice restaurant. Ladies go with a dress or skirt/pant combo you're comfortable with and gentlemen should go with a seasonal suit that reflects what time of day the event is taking place.

CASUAL

This means the event will likely be held outside, but jeans and shorts and tanks are likely not cool unless specified. Which is doubtful.

Ladies can opt for a more casual sundress or skirt-and-top ensemble.

Gentlemen can go with khakis, a button-down, and loafers of your choosing. Bring a blazer or a cardigan as well that you can eschew if others are going without.

CHAPTER 8

Health

"How do you manage to get it all done?" "A combination of multivitamins & rage usually powers me through the day."

Without our health, we have nothing. When you're sick and feel like crap, even with just the common, obnoxious cold, everything else in your life takes the backseat. That's why it's imperative to listen to your body and get a decent amount of sleep, not go on overextended benders, and actually get some fruits and vegetables in your system as opposed to the cyclical pattern of Chinese take out and pizza drunk munchies.

Because our healthcare system is currently more or less fucked, it's a lot cheaper and easier to lump the concept of self-care in with our overall health. Having an enviable complexion through a combinations of masks, toners and moisturizers is a fairly formidable accomplishment, but doesn't make up for blowing off going to the doctor in three years.

I'm not a medical professional, no matter how many of them have ghosted me over the years, so here are the basics, which essentially boil down to listen to your gut and seek professional help when something is physically, mentally, or emotionally off. Oh, and wear a condom.

SEXUALLY TRANSMITTED DISEASES*

Sex is fun. Sex is great. Sex is necessary for the survival of the human race. And as long as it's safe, you shouldn't feel guilty about it. The only things you should be concerned about regarding your sexual activity, aside from the emotions at stake, is not getting pregnant if you're not in the market for a kid at the moment, and doing your damnedest to not get any STDs.

Some of my more adventurous friends have never gotten anything, as if touched by the patron saint of DTF, and some of my more cautious friends have caught them, which seems wildly unfair. But STDs don't care about the number of partners you've had—it's the luck of the draw paired with the precautions you take. Just don't assume someone looks "safe"—that's your own bias blindly backing up your apathy towards condoms.

At the very least, you should be getting STD checks once a year. To be on the safe side, aim for every six months or so if you have multiple partners. Your health insurance should cover a physical every year, which will include STD tests. If you call your health insurance (which you really, really should do before getting any tests so you don't rack up a surprise bill) and they say you've fulfilled your yearly quota, get your ass to a public clinic if you can't afford it.

HOW WILL I KNOW IF A PAST PARTNER HAD A STD?

Either they'll have the guts to tell you, or a clinic will call you. If a former partner tests positive for an STD the doctor will have them write down the names and numbers of all their past partners in the time frame of the STD (or whomever they can remember) and someone from the clinic will call them so the person who contracted it will remain anonymous. There's also the very real chance they won't tell you, because people are assholes, so that's where your own testing comes in.

HPV (HUMAN PAPILLOMAVIRUS)

Well I have some good and bad news. As always, let's get the bad news over with first. You probably have HPV (and herpes, but that's for later). And now for the good news—so does everyone else.

According to my boyfriend, WebMD, "Nearly every sexually active person will have HPV at some point." You can even get it from skin-to-skin contact if there was no penetration whatsoever!

Most types of HPV have no symptoms and your body can get rid of it on its own, because it's in your body's best interest to stay alive and that thing works overtime. Some of the more unlucky symptoms of HPV include genital warts and those can also infect the mouth and throat.

> # If I have an STD it's only because I'm popular.

---

* Unless specified otherwise, all of the following info has been sourced from WebMD.

Even if there are no symptoms, HPV can cause cancer of the cervix, penis, mouth, or throat. There are vaccines that prevent the cancer and if you didn't get it while you were younger, hop on it now. Men are predominantly just carriers of HPV and never exhibit any symptoms or health problems, but should still get the vaccine as a precaution/to be nice to their female partners.

If you're female, your annual pap smear should check for HPV.

CHLAMYDIA
I thought HPV would be the most commonly reported STD in the US but it's actually Chlamydia. You predominantly contract Chlamydia through vaginal or anal sex but apparently oral sex can screw you over too.

Symptoms include odd discharge or a burning sensation when you pee, and that's when you know to get your ass to a doctor for prescribed antibiotics. Don't forget to get your partner(s) tested and treated too.

GONORRHEA
Sometimes you get the one, two sucker punch—Chlamydia *and* Gonorrhea (you lucky duck)! Gonorrhea has the same symptoms as Chlamydia (unusual discharge and burning when you pee) although men usually exhibit symptoms and women don't.

Doctor-prescribed antibiotics will clear that right up.

SYPHILIS
Syphilis is a really fun one. It starts out with a sore that can look as innocuous as an ingrown hair, cut or random bump. Then it turns into a body rash and sores in your mouth, vagina, or anus. Untreated syphilis can lead to organ, nerve, and brain damage, which was a real issue a couple of centuries ago.

Now, luckily, syphilis is easily treatable with antibiotics. Needless to say the earlier you get to your doctor, the better.

HERPES
Unlike the other STDs on this list, Herpes is a virus so it can't be cured. It's also super easy to catch because it's spread by skin-to-skin contact, so even if you wear a condom you can still contract it. People are most contagious when they're having a herpes breakout with visible blisters, but you can still catch it with no blisters present.

Most of the time doctors won't even check you for Herpes unless you're exhibiting symptoms because you probably already have it and they don't want to freak you out with a positive diagnosis.

The main symptoms of herpes are literally painfully obvious—uncomfortable blisters around the penis, vagina, or anus. You might even have them inside your vagina or anus where you can't feel them.

Herpes can be managed with medication, but there's no magical cure yet. Which is why it's super important to always use condoms—better safe than sorry.

HIV/AIDS

HIV was essentially a death sentence a few years ago, but thank God there are now ways to combat and treat it.

HIV is passed on through bodily fluids, like blood, semen, vaginal fluids, and breast milk. You can catch it by sharing needles, or having sex without a condom. You can't get HIV from saliva, so kissing is totally cool.

There are daily pills you can now take that help prevent you from contracting HIV, and if you're concerned about getting it then by all means get a prescription.

✚ WHEN DO YOU CALL AN AMBULANCE AND WHAT SHOULD YOU EXPECT WHEN THE PARAMEDICS ARRIVE?

Aside from strippers dressed as paramedics and firefighters, I've (thankfully) not had much experience in the emergency medicine department.

With that in mind I asked former NYC paramedic Garrett McCarthy on when you should actually call an ambulance, and what to expect when the paramedics or EMTs show up.

> "Paramedics and EMTs are a lot like public bathrooms. You don't generally notice them until you need them, and when you need them, it's usually an emergency.
>
> There are countless bona fide reasons to request an ambulance, and if you really feel that pit in your stomach that screams 'something isn't right here' just call 9-1-1. The worst that can happen is you get two EMTs or Paramedics who show up, assess the situation, and advise the next steps in the process. You won't be reprimanded for calling, even if it turns out to be something minor...

In a related vein (pun intended), here are some tips for when you should dial 9-1-1:

- When a concerning quantity of blood has suddenly appeared outside the body.
- When air stops going in to the body.
- When someone who should be awake is no longer awake or rousable.

I don't think, "What doesn't kill you only makes you stronger," applies to last night.

- When a sudden change in mental status is noticed and you generally have no idea of the cause.
- When a person is unable to move themselves due to sickness or injury.
- Any other time you are uncomfortable handling a medical situation or emergency.

Contrary to the above, there are some instances where calling an ambulance isn't advisable. (Important side note: any paramedic or EMT who intends to keep their job will never tell you to not call an ambulance, since the liability in saying that is a surefire way to a lawsuit.) The following are instances where you might want to rethink your need to dial the 'I'm dying' number and maybe break out the Uber app:

- Bleeding that can be managed with a Band-Aid (think: paper cuts)
- Orthopedic injuries that don't render you incapable of movement (think: stubbed toes)
- General illness attributable to a known cause (think: your three roommates have the flu and now you're getting a fever)
- Chronic pain or sickness (anything you've had for a significant amount of time)

People tend to think of emergency rooms as clinics, and ambulances as free rides but there are substantial bills for both. Alternatively, a $12 Uber ride and a $35 copay at a clinic is a much easier pill to swallow (again, pun intended). Consider heading to a local clinic over the ER if things aren't plainly emergent, but again: I would never advise you to refrain from calling 9-1-1 if you believe that is the correct thing to do."

BOOBS AND BALLS SELF-EXAMS + IDENTIFYING UTIS

BREAST SELF-EXAM

One in eight women will be diagnosed with breast cancer in their lifetime. It's a scary statistic, and one that affects all of us. You're more at risk when there's family history involved, but you should be doing monthly breast self-exams regardless, if only for your own peace of mind. According to Johns Hopkins Medical Center, "Forty percent of diagnosed breast cancers are detected by women who feel a lump, so establishing a regular breast self-exam is very important." If you notice any breast tissue changes, call your doctor immediately. Thankfully, eight out of ten lumps are not cancerous but it's still imperative to get it checked out as soon as possible.

On that note I once asked a medical student I was seeing if he could check me for lumps and he said something along the lines of, "No you idiot it's not foreplay, it's uncomfortable if you check yourself correctly."

There are several ways you can perform a self-breast exam, care of the National Breast Cancer Foundation Inc.

- **In the shower**
  Using your fingers, move around your entire breast from the outside to the interior in a circular motion, checking the entire breast and armpit area for lumps or anything that feels hard or thick (that's what she said).

- **In front of a mirror**
  Check out your boobs with your arms at your sides, and then with your arms raised high overhead.

  Look for any visual changes like swelling, dimpling of the skin or nipple changes. Then, place your palms on your hips and press firmly down to flex your chest muscles and look again for any conspicuous changes.

- **Lying down**
  Your boobs spread out more evenly while you're lying down, so this makes it easier to check. Place a pillow under your right shoulder and place your right arm behind your head. Using the pads of your fingers on your left hand, feel around your right breast in a circular motion covering the entire breast and armpit using light, medium and firm pressure. Squeeze your nipple (ouch, I know) to check for discharge and lumps. Repeat on your left breast.

"What are you up to today?" "Self-care." "So you ordered the extra bagel, then."

CHECKING YOUR BALLS FOR CANCER

Testicular cancer is the second most common cancer for men, second to skin cancer. According to the American Cancer Society sometimes there are no symptoms, but a painless swelling or lump on your balls is a big clue. Some less common symptoms include your balls changing size and shape, overall feeling of heaviness in your scrotum, pain down there and in the abdomen, and enlarged nipples.

One of the best ways to catch testicular cancer is regular checks, preferably right when you get out of the shower and your testes are warm, relaxed and hang lower.

- Use the palm of your hand to support the scrotum and pay attention to the size and weight for future reference. It's totally normal for one of your balls to hang lower or be larger.

- Gently roll a ball between your thumb and fingers, feeling for any lumps in or on the surface. Your balls should feel firm and smooth.

- Find the epididymis—a coiled structure at the back of your penis that transfers sperm from the balls to the penis—and use your fingers and thumb to check for any lumps.

- Repeat with the other ball.
- If you find anything, hightail your ass to a doctor.

URINARY TRACT INFECTIONS

If you've ever had the pleasure of experiencing a UTI, you'll know it. You constantly feel like you need to pee and when you finally do, it hurts like hell. While you're experiencing UTI symptoms it's hard to concentrate on anything else, and being at work just adds a whole other layer to how wholly terrible they are.

Urinary tract infections occur when bacteria enters the urinary system through sex or wiping issues. While men can get UTIs, women are extremely susceptible to their hellish presence. The female urethra is two inches long while the male's is eight to nine inches, so it has nothing to do with how clean you are, just the way our bodies work.

If you constantly have to pee, it really hurts when you do, or it's cloudy or foamy, that's most likely a UTI. If it's accompanied with clumpy, cottage-cheese-like discharge (great visual!) it's probably a yeast infection. If there's other strange discharge along with sores and bleeding, it's probably a STD.

But wait, it gets more fun! If you have a fever, chills, nausea, or back pain, it may have spread to your kidneys and you have a kidney infection. It's rare, but it can happen, and is totally treatable with a doctor's visit and a full round of antibiotics.

UTIs can get better on their own after 10-14 days because the human body is nothing but miraculous (except when it wants to self-destruct), but unless you're a severe masochist, get your ass to a doctor where they can prescribe you antibiotics that will kick in within 24-36 hours. You'll take 3-5 days of meds, which you will need to take in full even when the symptoms disappear.

HOW DO I PREVENT UTIS?

Peeing before foreplay or sex and after sex is always a good rule, along with wiping from front to back. Also, try to avoid vaginal sex after anything anal or just scrub up before you go back to ol' fashioned vaginal penetration. Once you've had even just one UTI, the fear of getting one again will supersede any awkwardness with a partner.

OVER THE COUNTER OR HOME REMEDIES

There are over-the-counter medications that help mask the symptoms, but your best bet is getting some damn antibiotics. I am extremely pro medication, if you haven't noticed.

The sugar-free cranberry juice method is inconclusive, but anything you're drinking to make you pee should help. You should try to stay away from alcohol, coffee, caffeinated sodas, artificial sweeteners, spicy foods, and acidic fruits that rub your bladder the wrong way while you're on meds.

Also, abstain from sex during this time. It will be anything but pleasant and can push more bacteria into the already infected area.

TL;DR: get your ass to a doctor as soon as you see the warning signs of a UTI. If you can't afford the co-pay or don't have insurance (God bless the American healthcare system/please hit me up if you're an attractive Canadian male), over-the-counter meds and mainlining water should help.

ANXIETY—HOW TO IDENTIFY AND TREAT IT

Everyone has varying degrees of anxiety whether they admit to it or not. Anxiety becomes an issue when it weaves itself into your everyday life, becoming the new normal and affecting everything from your work performance to social life.

Anxiety has become a lot more prevalent because of our access to worldwide news, and the constant barrage of all the horrible things happening in the world would make anyone feel sick. I was physically ill for a good part of the 2016 election cycle because I was working in a newsroom and was not only privy to the destruction it wreaked on our country, but was required to pay attention to it. The mind/body connection is real, never discount that.

Symptoms of something more than fleeting anxiety include:

- Feelings of dread or panic
- Nervousness and restlessness or insomnia
- Rapid heart rate or breathing
- Gastrointestinal problems
- Difficulty focusing on anything other than the thing you have anxiety about
- Symptoms of OCD (obsessive compulsive disorder) or PTSD (post-traumatic stress disorder). OCD is when you're performing certain tasks over and over again and PTSD is when the anxiety surrounds an experience that happened in the past.

If you're riddled with anxiety then you can succumb to panic attacks. Panic attacks are terrifying and include a sudden onset of some of these symptoms:

- Shaking and trembling
- Excessive sweating
- Heart palpitations

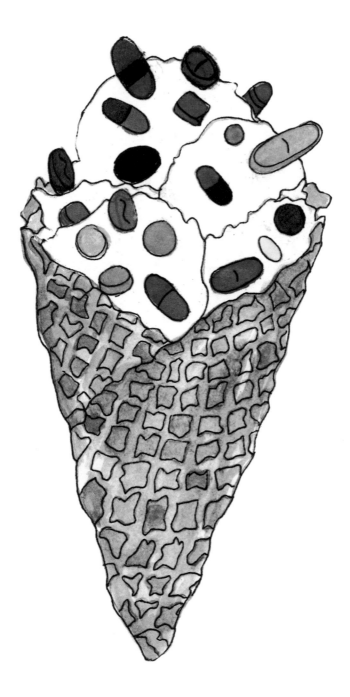

"Mmmmm, multivitamins."

"Rearranging my cocktail and black tie dresses is its own form of therapy," she said to the stray cat looking up at her from the alley. The cat thought it was too early for the girl to start drinking.

- Shortness of breath or feeling like you're being choked
- Feeling really hot or cold
- Dizziness, feeling light-headed, or that you're going to faint
- Fear of going crazy or dying
- Nausea or gastro problems
- Feeling detached from yourself, as if you're watching it all happen

Oftentimes people with panic attacks will head to the emergency room because they think they're suddenly extremely sick. You are ill, but it's a result of everything you're mentally and emotionally dealing with and need to seek psychiatric help.

ANXIETY TREATMENT

If you're persistently feeling any of the above anxiety symptoms or have experienced a panic attack, get your ass to a doctor or therapist. Preferably the latter, but if you're worried about therapy co-pays then your general practitioner can prescribe medication (likely a SSRI) for anxiety. However if you're taking medication you should really complement it with therapy.

DEPRESSION

We all feel depressed sometimes. Whether a relationship ended, you're dealing with the loss of a family member or friend, or the weight of life's decisions have gotten you down, feeling like complete shit is normal and even expected. Especially when you're dealing with the clusterfuck that is post-grad life.

With that said, if you persistently exhibit the following symptoms of

"Refuse to be anything less than inspired by the world around you," she said with a twirl of her vibrant skirt.

"So that will be a large chili and small fry? And miss we can't 'spike' the Diet Coke," said the Wendy's cashier.

depression, get your ass to a doctor.

- Fatigue
- Trouble concentrating and making decisions
- Feeling worthless, guilty, or helpless
- General pessimism or hopelessness
- Overeating or loss of appetite
- Feeling empty
- Constant existential crises
- Persistent digestive problems that won't respond to treatment
- Insomnia, sleeping too much, waking up wayyy too early
- Suicidal thoughts

Once you make an appointment, your doctor will ask:

- When the symptoms started
- How long they've lasted
- If mental illness runs in your family
- If you have a history of drug or alcohol abuse (yup, including "casual" abuse during college)

The doctor may then start treatment, refer you to a mental health professional, or both. A lot of the people I know swear by a mix of the two so you're getting both the in-person and prescription elements.

WARNING SIGNS OF SUICIDE

There's nothing poetic about suicide and your quickly and unceremoniously exiting the situation doesn't solve a problem. It creates a shitload more for the people that love and want the best for you.

In the past few weeks of writing this there have been several prominent celebrity suicides, highlighting that even the people who really do have it all can still be wildly depressed, and money, fame, family, and fans don't always help.

Only you will know if you're having suicidal thoughts, and it's up to you to get the professional help you need. But if you see a friend, coworker, or loved one exhibiting any of the following behaviors, for the love of God, take action and at the very least talk to them about it.

- A sudden switch from their acting depressed to being very calm or happy (this is when they've decided they're going to go through with it and have an exit strategy, so to speak)
- Taking risks like jaywalking into traffic or driving through red lights
- Constantly speaking about being absolutely worthless or hopeless
- Talking about suicide or "wanting out"
- Making or editing their will, getting affairs in order
- Always thinking about death
- Visiting or calling loved ones

YOUR FRIENDS ARE NOT THERAPY

As much as your friends love and want the best for you, they are (usually) not licensed therapists. And if they are, you should be paying them for their trouble.

Everyone has their own problems and issues even if they're not electing to talk about them, and while your friends are great, empathetic listeners, it's exhausting to hear your litany of problems for happy hours on end. Feel free to share your troubles openly, but just remember that their listening to your complaining shouldn't be the driving factor of your friendship. Similarly, if you feel like a friend does nothing but complain to you, gently suggest they seek professional help and try to change the subject. They should get the point.

WARNING SIGNS FOR DRUG AND ALCOHOL ABUSE

A lot of us have had a moment in our literal darker hours, using blackout shades and any and every hangover cure possible while wondering, "Do I

"Where am I? What happened?"

"Miss, we found you in the fetal position in Whole Foods while cradling a charcuterie platter."

have a problem?" It's a scary thought, but sometimes a plausible one.

Life is easier with a buzz and when things aren't going exactly as planned, news and a modified outlook are easier to take in when you're even just slightly fucked up.

The following warning signs aren't an "oh God I'm never drinking again" type of feeling, but ones where your body is crying out in pain because it's craving alcohol to function.

- Blackouts or memory loss
- Recurring fights
- Depression, irritability
- A cycle of using alcohol to cheer up, feel better, sleep, feel normal, etc.
- Drinking in the mornings, in secret, and alone
- Really terrible, persistent hangovers whenever you stop drinking
- Red face, black and tarry stools, chronic diarrhea, vomiting blood, trembling hands, husky voice

Addiction clearly isn't just related to alcohol, and vices like heroin, meth, coke, and various party drugs can quickly become an extremely hard habit to kick. Not to mention, can immediately kill you.

Signs of addiction either to drugs or alcohol include:

- Complete loss of control, or using even though you intend not to
- Neglecting activities or hanging out with people in favor of using
- Taking risks to obtain what you're using
- Foregoing maintaining your appearance
- Having issues maintaining relationships
- Having a scarily high tolerance while trying to get drunk or high
- Going through withdrawal if you're not using (irritability, depression, anxiety, nausea or vomiting, loss of appetite, headaches, sweating, fatigue)

- Continuing using even when you're experiencing the above, and it's having a negative impact on your life

"K," an acquaintance, is now sober but has a history of alcohol and drug abuse and was kind enough to highlight when he knew he had to stop.

"I was addicted to drugs and alcohol, mostly drugs. I knew it had to stop while I was at my parent's house with my sister and girlfriend, and my sister was yelling at me, telling me I was a coward. That so many people love me and I was putting them through hell.

I left the house and started walking but couldn't go far because I was too tired, both physically and emotionally. And that's when I knew I had to go to rehab."

"Can you please clean your crushed pills off the cheeseboard next time? Your cousins noticed."

YOUR SKINCARE REGIMEN

Skincare has blown up in recent years because thanks to the constant barrage of depressing news it feels like the world is on fire and you're otherwise helpless to stop it. But at the very least you can have camera-ready skin thanks to an array of indulgent, accessible products that will make you feel better in the moment! And who among us hasn't taken a sheet mask selfie?

Because I'm the worst at skincare and will just use whatever I have on hand or restock my cabinet with drug store products, I asked Micaela English, writer and adult acne survivor, about a universal skincare regimen.

"Reality check: you will never look as young, and hydrated, and wrinkle-free as you do now. Like ever. So take a camera roll worth of selfies. However, there are plenty of magic potions (of the beauty counter variety) that can help you look your best as you creep into your late 20s.

CLEANSER
The most important step of your skincare routine. If you don't have clean skin...you're screwed. The amount of pollution, and disgusting who knows what, that ends up on your face on a daily basis is horrifying.

TREATMENT
Have a first round interview at your dream job and a cherry red zit on the middle of your forehead? Been there. The reality is, acne happens to all of us, but it is exasperated during times of stress, when you're partying, and not eating right. If acne is a constant struggle, I can't stress enough

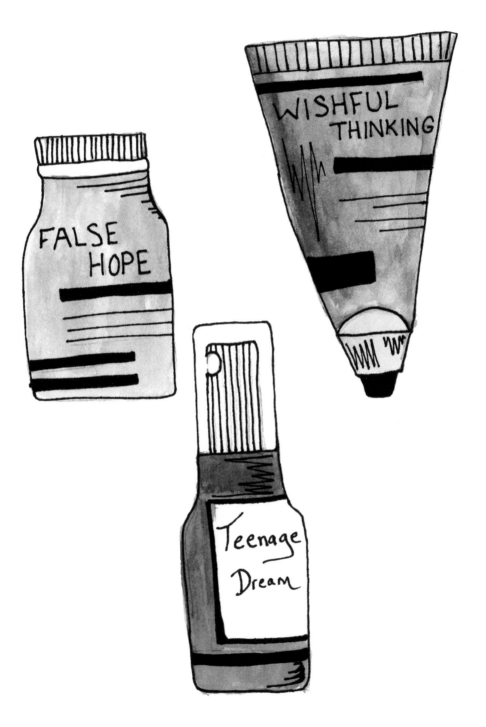

that you should go to the dermatologist and get topical treatments to help. Maybe your skin is super hormonal, or it has something to do with your diet, but a dermatologist will help steer you in the right direction.

MASK

After a night out, your skin probably looks like the sh*t emoji.

A quick fix: a face mask. Sheet masks are easy, hydrating, and there's no mess to wash off in the sink.

EYE CREAM

In my opinion your eyes are the first to show signs of aging (if that's what you want to avoid of course) and you should combat that with eye cream.

SPF

Take it from someone in their 30s who has sun damage....SPF does make a difference. UV rays are stronger than ever and your friends that look hot from a Montauk tan now will be wrinkly in a few years. SPF is a non-negotiable.

DAY AND NIGHT CREAM

Yes, your day cream can be the same as your night cream. But the reality is that when you sleep your skin regenerates and you may want to pack a bigger moisture and recovery punch than during the day."

> "Self-care Sunday!" She yelled into the tastefully decorated void.

EXERCISE, A NECESSITY 📢

Welcome to the years when your metabolism is starting to slow down. You could be spending late nights at work and your job covers meals if you stay past a certain time and your sanity is craving a cheesesteak. You could just be more sedentary than you'd like between a desk job and the constant allure of screen time. Who hasn't parked themselves in front of a TV for the day with all the snacks you could ever need?

This is where the desperate need for exercise comes in, if not for your waistline, then for your lifespan. According to a 2017 study in the *Lancet*, "Getting only two and a half hours of weekly exercise was associated with a 28 percent reduction in premature death, and a 20 percent reduction in heart disease."

And this isn't two and a half hours of intense workouts. Dr. Scott Lear, the study lead author noted to *Vox*, "Our findings indicate that nonrecreational activity—work, housework, active transportation—is just as beneficial in reducing the risk for premature death and heart disease."

"This offends my delicate sensibilities."

"Ma'am, we're legally required to show the bagel calories."

So while SoulCycle, Equinox, Barry's Bootcamp, and other luxury workout spaces are all the rage (and honestly the new way to show off that you can afford such extravagances without being overtly gauche), even just walking to work will help you immensely.

I asked Brooke Danielson, Fashion and Lifestyle Director for *SHAPE* magazine, about her thoughts on working out on a budget.

"Working out can be fun, yes fun! It doesn't need to cost an arm and a leg to do so. So long as you can move and get your heart rate up you are technically working out. Forget the fancy gym memberships, expensive classes, and any workout that has you buying tons of gear. It's as simple as going for a run outside, learning yoga and practicing in your living room, streaming a dance class from YouTube or taking a long walk and doing push-ups after. The most important thing you can do for yourself is take care of yourself, so find a workout you *like*. To Hell with 'like' actually, find a workout you *love*. When you find a workout that clicks you are more likely to stick to the routine. Trust me, from someone who has tried many different classes and methods of cardio, strength training, etc...so long as you love the workout you are doing it won't feel like work. Now, ditch the money-draining gyms and try to enjoy nature a bit more. Put your phone down, be present, and have fun."

CHAPTER 9

Personal
Brand

You finally meet your personal brand in Hell.

Whenever I see the words "personal brand," my bullshit meter goes off the charts. Who you are and what you stand for can't be neatly, aesthetically packaged, but it sure as hell looks that way on social media.

Aside from deciding how thotty your Instagram should look, there are multiple ways of determining what you want your "personal brand" to be (which is really just unnecessary marketing jargon for how you want to be perceived by the world). In today's internet culture and with the way hiring works, it's not a bad idea to present yourself as someone who seems like a competent, professional human being that also has an active social life. The latter is so you can still have fun with social media and engage with your friends and hot strangers, but also shows that you're "normal" and have potential to be a team player.

You're probably inherently doing this across your social platforms by maintaining:

- A professional looking LinkedIn
- A friendly appearing Facebook (preferably locked or with any underage or embarrassing drinking photos untagged or deleted)
- A "fun" Instagram page that stylistically highlights how you want to be perceived
- A Twitter bereft of nasty commentary or trolling

"Of course I already have all that." You say, taking another swig of Bud Light and adding the can to the growing pyramid on your IKEA coffee table. "But what the hell is my personal brand? How can I define something that for all intents and purposes is either fluid as I grow and mature as a person or is otherwise fabricated?" Well my friend, let's take some steps to identify what makes you unique. And you should probably recycle that beer tower before it starts to smell.

How to define your personal brand (with as little self-loathing as possible)

What makes you unique and authentic? Are you a no nonsense, no BS hard worker? A globe-trotting thrill seeker? An unapologetic animal lover? A health nut with the abs to prove it?

This is where you have to be clear about who you are—what you see in yourself and what you want others to see you. By creating a story arc and sticking to it, this is how you build yourself up as an individual with dedicated space in this world.

If you don't necessarily know what you want your "thing" to be, not to worry! Ask yourself:

- What do I consider my greatest success?
- What skills have I used to overcome formerly near-impossible obstacles?
- What comes easier to me than most people?
- What do I value most?
- What topics do I get excited and talk a lot about?

You should have some clarity about what you're good at and passionate about, but if you want alternative opinions ask your more truthful loved ones. Not your grandparents who love literally anything and everything you do, or your significant other who was planning on seeing you naked later and doesn't want to piss you off today. You want your personal brand to be rooted in authenticity (insert jerking off motion here), and that begins with being honest with yourself concerning your strengths and weaknesses.

By pinpointing what makes you talented and unique, you can now start tackling how to best showcase and exhibit those special traits in a non-douchey way. Your personal brand is little more than a packaged collection that infers what you consider your strengths, values, and passions.

It all boils down to:

- Whose attention are you trying to get?
- What authentic story are you trying to tell?
- Why are you doing this: for you career, fun, or both?

With those three questions in mind, it's time to put an actionable plan in motion.

IF THIS IS FOR EMPLOYERS

By creating a cohesive social media presence that reflects who you are as a person both aesthetically and in your tonality and voice, employers have a better idea of "who you are" and why they should hire you. Aggregating past examples of your work (even if it was just spec or student projects) on a clean site that connects to your LinkedIn and any presentable social media platforms makes it seamless and easier for hiring managers to check you out. And your making their lives easier will make them more likely to call you.

If you don't have a PC social media presence, or have one that you'd be embarrassed for a potential boss to look at—then put it on lockdown. Social media first impressions count more than you think among the younger set, especially if you're interviewing or auditioning for a marketing, branding, or creative role. For example, a brand I was freelancing for hired a new manager I had to report to. Of course the team looked at her Instagram and it was uh, *a lot*. I'm talking ass shots poolside in Vegas, full fishnet outfits, and all the fake Girl Boss paraphernalia you can find littering the clearance aisles at Marshall's. Whenever I looked at her or had to do what she said, that painful imagery and tone-deaf captions were all I could think about.

IF THIS IS SOLELY FOR SOCIAL PURPOSES

Then have at it. Post whatever interests you and makes you look good (a thirst trap is such an underrated ego boost!) without calling so much attention to yourself that people will go out of their way to screenshot and jeopardize your career and relationships. It's the wild, wild west of digital out there and the internet is forever—protect yourself wherever and whenever you can.

IF IT'S A MIX OF BOTH

This is what most people cater to—content that's both a social and creative outlet that won't get them fired if their locked accounts are screenshot.

> "I'm going to start a lifestyle & career blog called 'aspirational loungewear.'"

Or you have a socially acceptable Instagram you keep unlocked to make you look more rounded to employers. If you look good on paper *and* you seem like you have friends, it all complements one another in your best interests.

Caveat: *never, ever, ever* refer to your "personal brand" out loud except in a joking manner. It's tasteless to the point of being offensive and people will mock you—and rightly so!

BLOGGING/INFLUENCERS/TASTEMAKERS

At the core of it, social media is an escape. An opportunity to glance at a world outside your own with incredible foods to eat, insanely gorgeous places to explore, beautiful or stylish people to look like—it's a reminder that your options are limitless and there's so much waiting for you outside your day-to-day life. And brands are more than aware of that, hopping onto bloggers' audiences

An example of the author's personal brand.

and aesthetics for a slice of more organic advertising.

Alice Wright, Founder of GOMIBLOG, noted, "Blogging, microblogging, and social media is the natural evolution of the reality show culture we grew up in. The fame achieved by people on Instagram or through blogging is similar to what used to be called the 'celebutante' phenomenon, or what Neal Gabler called 'human entertainment'—you can become famous simply for existing and being in the public eye."

So how does one become an influencer? By crafting a unique personal brand that people want to interact with and follow for their own reasons. Either because they appreciate your style and want to emulate you, or you give them a new worldview they're not accustomed to. It's harder to become a successful influencer now than it was several years ago when the market wasn't overly saturated with every kind of tastemaker. The bloggers I paid attention to back in 2006–2010 are now media powerhouses with their own merchandise, because the early adopters got their shit together first and profited off it. Those slots have been taken and it's getting harder and harder to be heard above the noise.

Right now it seems like everyone is an influencer or aspiring to be one, whether or not they're actually #sponsored. Sure, being an influencer or tastemaker seems like a great job to anyone paying attention to heavily sponsored content. Free trips, events, and products, plus fistfuls of cash in exchange for carefully curated photos and showing up to events seems like the dream, but it's harder than it looks. Behind the scenes there are mood boards, analytics, and agencies pouring money into certain influencers to hit specific demographics. And if you don't hit their numbers, you're no longer getting money; just free product. (Which really doesn't sound that bad unless it's your main source of income.)

If an influencer can't survive off promotions alone (or they don't want to) they can work for a brand or agency that understands their online persona and influence is akin to a portfolio—they have the talent and tools to get people to pay attention. This is how a lot of my friends make their living, while continuing to blog and promote for other brands on their own time.

I personally don't advocate your diving head first into attempting to be an influencer without a plan, reasoning, and set goals. And realizing you're probably going to need a lot of cash and time to make these things happen. Alice continues, "Most of those who make it to the highest rungs of blogging fame started with the same package as Paris Hilton or any Kardashian—they had the money, looks, and connections to back their climb, and the ability to hire people to navigate the business end of celebrity life. If you don't have those assets you are going to need a hook if you are going to get any traction. That's why there's still room for the Gosselins and Honey Boo Boos."

At the crux of it, why do you want to be an influencer? Because it looks like fun? You want free trips and products and attention? You have to work hard for that, and pinpoint how and why people will pay attention. Which takes us to:

The second rule of Fight Club is to never refer to yourself as an influencer.

NOT EVERYTHING HAS TO BE A SIDE HUSTLE

Do you enjoy a hobby or activity and are so proud of yourself and your work that you want to share it with the world? Cool, that's great! Do you need to create a whole lifestyle brand around it? For the love of God, no.

For example, If you're really into baking and want to make an Instagram or blog for your culinary creations, don't feel the need to pour everything into getting it sponsored by brands and becoming the next big foodie blogger with their own Target diffusion line and time slot on Food Network. It's not practical and will make you unnecessarily exhausted, turning a creative outlet you once loved into something you resent.

According to pWc's guide to personal branding, this very concept at a deeper level means you enjoy taking the raw, base ingredients and turning them into something great that you can share with others. How does that translate to your career and unlocking other skill sets you weren't necessarily aware of? You can still use this hobby to your gain outside the kitchen and not everything has to be a production for thousands of anonymous followers.

DELETE. DELETE. DELETE. ✖

One of the most important parts of having an online presence, regardless of its size, is deleting *anything* that can come back to bite you in the ass. That includes illegal, offensive, tasteless, truly embarrassing, or poorly thought out content. We see it playing out all the time on the news—public posts are used as evidence against people and quotes and images are lifted directly off any and all social platforms that aren't locked. Think of periodically sifting through the past and deleting the less savory bits as performing necessary maintenance, a form of botox for your digital presence if you will.

I don't envy the younger set (you guys) who've had an audience the entire time you've been posting bits and pieces of your lives. Back in my day, when I had a flip phone and could only use Twitter on desktop, anything stupid I posted didn't have an audience because social media outside of Facebook wasn't a widespread concept yet. Now you can delete as quickly as you possibly can, but someone could have already screenshot it because audiences are paying attention and social media has higher stakes.

"On this day" apps are useful in this respect because they show you what you said or did in the past, and if you don't like that day's content from say, three years ago, you can easily delete it without sifting through your archives. Some people I know regularly delete their entire timelines to save

"Another one bites the dust," she muttered, seeing another longwinded FB post about someone quitting their job to focus on their blog, seven years too late.

themselves the hassle of purging inappropriate content, and I have to admit, I've subscribed to this method as well.

THE DEFINITION OF "PERSONAL BRAND" AS DESCRIBED BY "INFLUENCERS"

I asked some aesthetically on-point influencers how they maintain an authentic personal brand:

"First off, I would never be so vulgar as to describe myself as having a 'personal brand.' If you want to define yourself, do the exact opposite of creating a 'personal brand.' Defining yourself is rooted in authenticity: being yourself for good, bad, or really bad. Granted this is more easily said than done, but everyone has something that makes them different. Find that...then exploit it. The rest comes naturally."

—Dean Zacharias, *@dean_m_z*

"Simply, people start following Instagram accounts because the accounts offer something different from what they already find in their feeds. Whether its travel, food, or fashion related, you have to showcase it in a way that's different and more interesting than the Instagram accounts on the explore page.

For me, I believe a genuine style of content that reflects who I am works best on social media. It's something I've learned by managing social media for brands, too. Just because one type of content really woks for a brand or person doesn't mean that the same is going to work for you.

Social media has always been a hobby and when it comes to my 'personal brand,' I just post things that are true to myself. Social media has played an important role in my career. I've made lifelong friends and used it as a networking tool. It's introduced me to so many opportunities. But most importantly I've used it as a creative outlet to showcase people, places, and things that I like."

—Julia Shingler, *@juliashingler*

"Not to oversimplify it, but you need a general understanding of what followers want to see on their feed. I see a lot of aspiring influencers posting their commutes and daily work days. Not interesting. People want to use social media to escape from their lives.

I use social media as a tool for my career. Almost like a portfolio for my work. My social media following has opened some pretty incredible doors. It definitely makes people look at you in a different light. This has been the best and the worst element. I think professionals in my field see my following as a verification of my ability, which has put me in front of some very incredible people at a young age. I get an array of offers to promote products on my Instagram page and I turn down 99% of them. I wish I could tell these kids that posting pictures of themselves with the latest detox tea for $167 post-tax is not worth it for the longterm personal brand, even if their aunt does end up using their 15 percent off code.

For me, social media has always been a hobby. It started out that way and I've managed to keep posting a mix of personal and professional work. I know a couple of these girls are making seven figures directly from social media, but I think, for the masses, it's so much more valuable as a marketing tool for your professional life, if applicable."

—Sean Gale Burke, @*seangaleburke*

CHAPTER 10

Last Words

LIFE ADVICE FROM THOSE WHO KNOW BEST

You may have seen the following people on television, or read their books or magazines, or watched their movies, but they all have one thing in common—they were all your age at some point. I asked some people I admire for life advice they'd tell their younger selves, and the answers weren't disappointing.

"Get 'It' out of your system. That's right, after you finish college, do every wild, crazy, nutty, instantaneous, outrageous thing you can do because, like Bob Dylan says, 'when you got nothing you got nothing to lose.'

Go hard.

But don't go too hard like I did. Don't end up homeless, .22 caliber pistol in the glove box, fifth of Jack at your side, no health insurance, trying to see a doctor in a farm workers' medical clinic 'cause you have a yellow patch of skin the size of a Mercator projection of Greenland on your belly and you can't scrub it off.

This will be the only time for the rest of your life that you don't have any responsibilities, so enjoy it. But, unlike me, attempt to stay healthy.

And then, when you are sick of being out of control, you may not want to hear this bit of naked, rapacious capitalism, but it is time to go out and make as much money, legally, as you possibly can, even if requires you do something you don't want to do. If you have to go to grad school to do it, then go. Set a goal of how much money you think you need to have total freedom, where you can tell the truth without fear and then go full stop when you hit that goal and not one penny more. You will then be as close to true happiness as possible.

If you do not have the financial wherewithal you will not be able to enjoy life and you will not be able to help others in need, which is the definition of real success. My philosophy works if you start out poor. If you are rich just skip phases one and two and go right to three."

—Jim Cramer, host of CNBC's *Mad Money with Jim Cramer* and co-anchor of CNBC's *Squawk on the Street*

"I think the best thing you can do when you move to a city in your twenties is to take in as much as you can. You'll never have as much energy and open-mindedness as you do at that time. So go drinking, get cheap tickets to the opera, give money to an arts organization (even if it's not much), become a regular at a bar, take up an off-beat sport (lawn bowling, anyone?), get closer to the people you find interesting. And get personalized stationery and send thank you notes the next day."

—David Coggins, writer and *NYT* best-selling author

"I would definitely tell myself not to be so panicked about finding my
dream job. I had so many hard jobs before I started my own company where
I was bored, felt underpaid, and was even doing jobs I knew I never wanted
to make a career out of, but they were all life experiences that lead to my
career today. There is so much pressure to find a good career right out of
college, but I didn't find my lifelong career or passion until over 10 years
later. If you're currently in job you dislike, or even dread, just remember it's
not a waste of time, and try to use every day to learn as much as you can to
take on with you. Don't like your manager? Even that is a lesson in learning
how to be a good manager and not do the things they do! I remember sitting
down with the finance department of my old job and asking how to use the
program they balanced the books with. They looked at me like I was crazy as
it was totally unrelated to my job—but then they showed me—and now I use
that program for the brand I started. It's only when you totally stop growing
personally or professionally within a job that you know it's time to move on.
Lastly, never be complacent and stay in any one job or in any relationship
that does not uplift, value, or treat you well."

—Myka Meier, founder of Beaumont Etiquette

"Outlast the bastards. All the horrible people you meet, including those
who look indestructible at the moment, will eventually hit the wall—in their
careers, in their marriages, plus some weight gain and hair loss too. You
may not be able to outrun them, out-dress them, outdo them, or out-party
them today, but you can outlast them. Think of a highway with wrecked cars
littering the grass on either side. And you're just cruising along gawking out
window as you slowly pass them all by.

Your mom and dad probably told you not to compare yourself to other
people. Well they were wrong. If you're not comparing yourself with other
people, then how do you know what the fucking score is?

The only thing on this earth that's undefeated is time. Think in terms of long
increments of time and you will win, even if it takes awhile."

—Joshua Brown, CEO of Ritholtz Wealth Management and CNBC contributor

"Here's the advice I'd give to myself: Say yes more. Say yes to everything
you reasonably can. Meet people who reach out to you and seriously
consider all inquiries and offers. Don't be so worried that things will be
bad or boring or hard or meaningless. They might be, but then again they
might not be. Send more unsolicited manuscripts and pitches, reach out to
more people for coffee, dream up more bad ideas. Don't start saying no and
getting serious until you absolutely have to."

—Elizabeth Angell, digital director of *Town & Country* and *Elle Decor*

"**Eat as many chocolate chip cookies as you can before hitting 25. Beyond** that age they won't taste the same, guilt will make sure of that. And your metabolism, deteriorating by the second, will pick up any slack on guilt's part. But you're not going to listen to any of this so I just completely wasted our time. I should've just told you LeBron will one day be a Laker. Now go celebrate by eating a cookie...I did. And as far as the career goes—continue to do the work but don't let the fear of uncertainty hinder the brief, fleeting moments of joy the work gives you. Figure out a way to love the process more than the end result."

—Justin Lader, screenwriter of *The One I Love* and *The Discovery*

"**My actual answer is probably something like 'for the love of God do not** sleep with [name redacted]' although I understand this is meant to be a universal exercise, so my second best piece of advice to my younger self is this: life is so much longer than you have any sense of right now. The thing about this time in your life is that everything, each decision and mistake and minor triumph, feels apocalyptic in ways you look back and laugh about later. Honestly, most of the shit you are doing right now doesn't matter nearly as much as you think it does—there is liberation and courage to be found in that."

—Brandy Jensen, social media director of *The Outline* where she also writes an advice column

"**I spent the majority of my 20s doing whatever I wanted. Between writing** and producing a zine (it was the 90s), hanging out at the Dovre Club with tough old guys including the likes of Warren Hinckle and occasionally Hunter S. Thompson, meeting Anton LaVey, acting, and, oh yeah, going to college every now and then. I pretty much did as I damn well pleased. My major regrets, if you can call them that, were the choices I made in relationships. Christ almighty, I picked all the wrong girlfriends, got married and divorced, and made the same mistakes over and over again well into my 30s, at which point I started making new stupid mistakes. It wasn't that they were bad people, it's that we were bad for each other. I always thought that relationships meant stability and fulfillment, which, of course, they do not. It all turned out OK—and if you just keep fucking going, it always does—but God, my relationships were just chaos. Well-intended, but you know what they say about the road to Hell.

At 44, I see my 24-year-old-self with a lot more detachment and empathy than I had in my 20s. I was fortunate in that I got and absorbed all the advice I needed then, so I'm not sure I would say anything to my younger self. I would, however, buy him a drink and say, 'Be kind to yourself: you have everything you need.' It's a mantra worth repeating as you navigate your way through your days, through your decades."

—K.S. Anthony, writer and editor

ACKNOWLEDGEMENTS

To say that this book is the product of many people is an understatement. In addition to the contributors, friends, and colleagues who so generously and thoughtfully gave me their time and expertise, I'd be remiss not to thank those without whose help this book would have remained a wishful thought.

Of course my family for literally, everything. Mom, Dad, Ben, Grandma, the Kasdan and Gordon clans; thanks for showering me with the love and support I don't really deserve. You're stuck with me so keep it up.

To the powerHouse Books team: Craig Cohen and Wes Del Val for giving a first-time author a shot, and Lizzi Sandell and Will Luckman for their incredible editing and patience.

To my friends for believing in me even when I didn't. I'd like to extend my gratitude to David Coggins, Emily Stewart, Ross Urken, Dan Kuhn, Hanna Howard, Shane Duggan, Brian Caggiano, Alexandra Beaton, Katrina Masterson, John Frelinghuysen and the rest of our lovely crew who either edited when they didn't need to, or made sure I saw the light of day while writing this. Love and G&Ts for all.

Sarah Solomon is the author and illustrator of *Guac is Extra But So Am I: The Reluctant Adult's Handbook*. She writes about style, personal finance, and emotional crutches for *The New Yorker*, *Town & Country*, *McSweeney's*, and others. She lives in NYC. Follow her on Twitter via @sarahsolfails or her self-parody account, @urbanJAP.

Author photo by Sean Gale Burke

COPYRIGHT

Published in the United States by powerHouse Books,
a division of powerHouse Cultural Entertainment, Inc.
32 Adams Street, Brooklyn, NY 11201-1021
e-mail: info@powerHouseBooks.com
website: www.powerHouseBooks.com

First edition, 2019

Library of Congress Control Number: 2019932215

ISBN 978-1-57687-913-9

Designed by Krzysztof Poluchowicz and Robert Avellan

Printed by Friesens Corp.

10 9 8 7 6 5 4 3 2 1

Printed and bound in Canada